QA
611.19
S76

Struble, Mitch
    Stretching a point

Stretching a Point

STRETCHING
A
POINT

by
Mitch Struble

A FRANKLIN INSTITUTE BOOK

THE WESTMINSTER PRESS
Philadelphia

ISBN 0–664–32499–1 (cloth)
ISBN 0–664–34002–4 (paper)

Library of Congress Catalog Card No. 74–155901

BOOK DESIGN BY DOROTHY ALDEN SMITH

Published by The Westminster Press ®
Philadelphia, Pennsylvania

PRINTED IN THE UNITED STATES OF AMERICA

Contents

Stretching a Point
Try It . . .

Take a point or a dot. What happens if you stretch it in one direction? Try it in your imagination, or else put the dot on a thin piece of rubber and really stretch it. The dot can actually be pulled into a line!

Now suppose you take the line and stretch it at right angles to its direction. The line becomes a flat surface. That's really stretching a point!

Believe it or not, what you have just done is a demonstration of a special kind of mathematics. This is what the following chapters are about, a fun kind of mathematics. You will meet some very odd experiences, like cutting down the middle of a piece of paper and having it remain in *one* piece, or finding that two loops can be separated without cutting one of them, or discovering that a doughnut has the same form as a teacup. You will need string, pencils, paper, and other easy-to-find odds and ends to perform simple experiments and problems in a branch of mathematics called "topology," the mathematics of form and shape.

In this book, topology is the study of lines, dots, sides, and edges in geometric figures, such as a triangle or a cube. We will be twisting, bending, stretching, and cutting these objects in a sort of rubber-sheet geometry. We will also explore the hole in a figure and how it changes things around it. Lines, dots, and figures have always had a great fascination for me. I hope this little book will give you some feeling of this wonder.

Directions for each project will tell you what materials to use and how to use them. It is important to follow the directions carefully, or results won't turn out as they should. Each problem is numbered. Some of the answers are in the main part of the book, others are in the back.

Trace or draw the figures on separate paper. If you do the puzzles in the book itself, you'll give away the answers to the next experimenter.

Get your pencils, paper, scissors, and string ready—here we go!

MITCH STRUBLE

1

Dots and Lines on Paper

We often hear that "the shortest distance between two dots is a straight line." Topology is not really concerned with the shortest distance or even the straightest line. Topology is concerned just with the fact that the two dots can be connected with a single line, whether it is straight or not. From now on, when we talk of a "line," we mean one that is *not* necessarily straight.

Think about three dots. How many lines are needed to connect each dot with the other two? It doesn't take much thinking to see that all we need is three lines. Each dot is connected to the other two without any line crossing another. We can use either straight lines or curved lines. The pictures show some of the ways to do this.

In topology, *all* are correct. You see that none of the lines cross. It doesn't matter how long they are, and it doesn't matter what the shape is. We say that such figures are *topologically equivalent*.

All the three-sided figures are members of what we call an *equivalence class*. The letters of the alphabet are, according to the topologist, made up of several equivalence classes. For example, the letter A has a hole and two separate tails on it.

What other letters have the same properties? Well, if you go through all the letters, the only one like the letter A could be the letter R. As you can see, it has a hole and two separate tails.

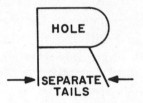

You could make your R a different way:

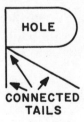

In this case, the two tails are connected, so the letter A is in an equivalence class by itself. The best way to decide what letters are members of an equivalence class is to think of the letters as being made of rubber so that they can be bent and stretched, but *not torn*. Let's try the equivalence class that includes the letter C. Put C on its back and stretch the sides, and it becomes the letter U. Twist it to make an S. Straighten it out and bend it once, and C can become an L or a V. Put two bends into it to make a Z or an N, or put three bends in it and make either

10

an M or a W. So, the equivalence class contains eleven members.

C I J L M N S U V W Z

See how many other equivalence classes there are for the capital letters. Try the small letters. Try the numerals 0 to 9. Remember that some of the letters or numerals can be written in different ways, such as the four (4 or 4). When you finish, see if you agree with the answers in the back.

Now, let's think about a piece of paper. We are going to call a part of the paper separated by lines a *region*. With a single line connecting two dots the piece of paper still has only one region, just as it had before the dots or line were drawn:

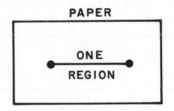

But now think of three dots and three lines. The new figure is enclosed, so that it forms one region and the rest of the paper is a second region. So three lines connected to three dots divide the paper into two regions.

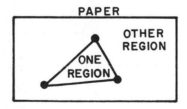

Try the following formula: Number of dots + number of regions − number of lines = ? For 3 dots, 2 regions, and 3 lines, your answer should be 2.

11

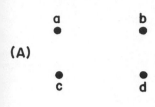

(A)

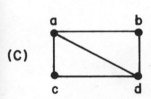

(B)

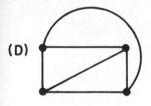

(C)

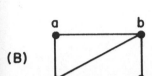

(D)

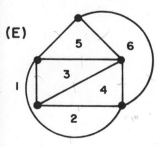

(E)

The formula was discovered by a Swiss mathematician named Leonhard Euler (Leo-nard Oil-er). He lived in the middle of the 1700's and has been called the "grandfather of topology." Actually, the name "topology" was not given to the subject we are studying until about a hundred years later! We will meet more of Euler's ideas later.

What can we do with four dots (A)?

Copy them on a sheet of paper. Now connect *all* the dots with each other so that *no* lines cross and then count the number of lines you need to do this and the number of regions you have. You will find that you can draw only five *straight* lines.

B or C is correct so far, but you have not connected dot *a* to dot *d* if your diagram looks like the first (B), or dot *b* to dot *c* if you drew it the second way (C). How are you going to do this? Reread the directions. Nothing was said about connecting the dots with *straight* lines! So use a curved line around the outside of the figure! *Six* lines are needed to connect *all* the dots to each other *without any crossing* (D).

Use the simple formula again: Dots + regions − lines = ? The number of dots is 4, the number of regions is 4 (Don't forget to count the outside area as one!), and the number of lines is 6. What number does the formula give you? Again, it is 2!

Because there are at most three lines meeting at a point, this is called a *network of degree three*. You have just found out three important properties about "lines" in topology. The first is that they do *not* have to be straight. The second is that they must *not* cross each other. The third is that they divide the paper into regions.

Now, let's add a fifth dot to our first four dots, as in E. The directions are the same. Connect each dot to all the other dots with lines that do not cross each other. Of course, some of the lines will not be straight. Try this for a while and then come back to the book.

Give up? You can't do it? Well, don't feel sad. No one else has done it either! You always end with a line that must cross another. The problem is impossible to do on a flat sheet of paper, but it can be done on a piece of paper with some curious properties that we shall construct later. We can still work with our five dots, though. Copy them again. Now connect as many as you can without any crossing and count the dots, lines, and regions. Your figure may look something like the drawing (E). Using the formula: 5 dots + 6 regions − 9 lines = 2, again!

To explore that formula a bit further, let's return to our three dots. If we add another line between two dots, how does it change the number of dots, lines, and regions? You can see that all it does is add one line and one region. The number of dots is the same. So, in our formula: 3 dots + 3 regions − 4 lines = 2, again!

Add another line between any two dots and use the formula again. The answer is still 2. If you look at the formula, you see that the number of dots stays the same. The number of regions increases by one and the number of lines also increases by one. So, when the number of lines is subtracted from the number of regions, the result is always the same. Try this with as many lines as you wish, as long as *none* cross!

Now let's see what happens when one line does cross another. Using three dots and letting one line cross another, your figure looks like the drawing. Up to this time we have been very careful about lines not crossing. Now that they are crossing, has something changed? Yes! You have to consider that the crossing is like a *new dot*. The original dots were like places where lines crossed or met one another. Now think in reverse: two lines crossing or touching form a dot. There is one more thing. Now our two lines become *four* lines, because they have been divided by the crossing, two lines on each side of the dot. Once you count the crossing as a dot, the formula still works: 4 dots + 4 regions − 6 lines = 2, again. Add to the figure another line that crosses—that means one extra dot and two extra lines. So, count the regions and use the formula.

Now let's try *six* dots. Instead of talking of dots and lines, we can make a story out of this problem. There are three houses on one side of the street, electric, water, and gas companies on the other side. The problem is to connect pipes from the three houses to each of the three utilities *without* any pipes crossing. Since this has to be done on a piece of paper, you can't get sneaky and go through and under the paper! Copy the picture, numbering the houses. (Start with gas, then water, then electric.) Try drawing

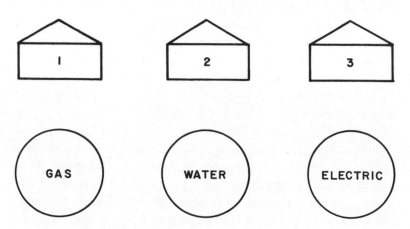

the connections for a while and then come back to the book.

Any luck? The same occurs as with the five dots. You can connect gas to all three houses, water to all three, but electric power to only two. You still have to find a way to connect electric to house #2. Since you could not connect five dots without any crossing, you probably suspected that you could not do it with six either. If we try to connect *all* six dots to each other, like trying to connect everything with telephone lines, the problem becomes worse!

As with the five dots, it is impossible to connect the six dots on a flat sheet of paper. But you can do it on a piece of paper we will make later. Not only will we be able to connect all the pipes so that none cross, but we can connect each house to every other without any crossing, and each utility to the others without any crossing!

Maybe an easier way of thinking of the problem is that all the dots are houses and all the lines telephone connections and each house must be connected to every other

14

house. We can still use our formula with our six dots. If you connect as many dots as you can without crossing any lines, as you did when you first tried to solve the problem, your figure will probably look something like the diagram. Using the formula: 6 dots + 8 regions − 12 lines = 2, again!

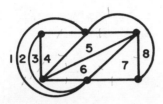

This formula will work with just about any network. It doesn't matter how you draw it, just as long as you count correctly. A formula that does not change from network to network is called an *invariant* (in-var-e-ant). This concept is very important in mathematics and science. An invariant is something that never changes, always staying the same in *any* situation.

2

The Koenigsberg Bridges and Networks

In the old kingdom of Prussia, which is now in East Germany, there was a city named Koenigsberg. (Today it is called Kaliningrad.) It was built where the Pragel River formed two islands and divided into two branches. Seven bridges connected the two islands to each other and to the opposite banks, very much like the picture.

A represents the northern
   sector of the town
B represents the island
C represents the southern
   sector of the town
D represents the eastern
   sector of the town

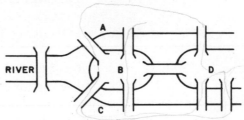

Most townspeople knew that all seven bridges could not be crossed on a continuous trip unless one bridge was *re-crossed*. The four letters in the diagram are the possible starting places. Copy the figure and see if you can make a continuous trip with the pencil over all the bridges just once and make a complete circuit. You are allowed to let the pencil lines cross anywhere *except* on the bridges. Try this for a while and then come back to the book.

You cannot do it? Let's see why. We can think of all the possible paths as a figure shaped like the diagram, p. 18, top. (Squares represent bridges.) The problem is to try to copy the figure without retracing any line.

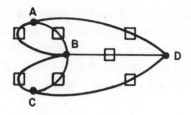

Your figure may look like the drawings below. (Try
starting at *A*— the order of the lines is numbered.)

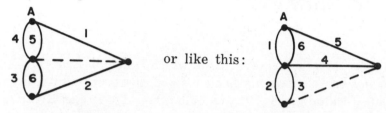

or like this:

You see that you cannot make a seventh line (dotted line
in figures) without retracing one line or lifting your pencil off the paper. This will happen no matter where you
start! You will always have a line left over that you cannot possibly draw without retracing at least one you have
already drawn.

Euler, whom you met earlier, figured out why this is so.
He called a dot, where the lines meet, a *vertex*. If an *even*
number of lines met there, he called it an *even vertex*. If
an *odd* number of lines met there, he called it an *odd vertex*. (When we talk of more than one vertex, we say "vertices".) He said if there are two odd vertices, or none, the
whole network *can* be drawn without any retracing. Let
us add a line connecting *A* and *C* as shown.

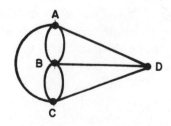

You can see that both *A* and *C* have an even number of lines meeting them now, in this case four lines. Now try starting at *D* and see if you can draw the figure without any retracing of the lines. We've drawn an answer with the paths numbered. This is not the only answer. There

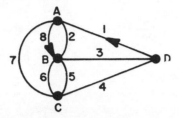

are five more. It would be interesting to see how many dif-

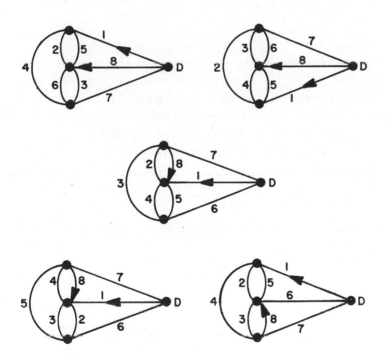

ferent ways you can draw this network without retracing any paths or taking your pencil from the paper. So far, we have started at *D*. Try starting at *B* and see what happens.

You will find that you *can* do it from *B* also. Here are four possible answers. (There are many more!)

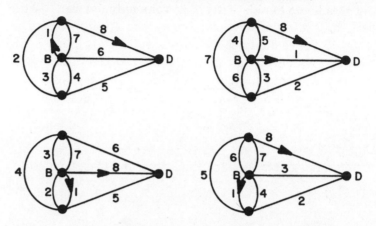

Now you may notice something about all of this. If you start at *D*, you always end up at *B*. If you start at *B*, you always end at *D*. Take a close look! In the first group, line #8 always ended at *B*. In the second group, line #8 always ended at *D*. You will notice that three paths meet at *D*, so it is an odd vertex. How many paths meet at *B*? Five, so it is also an odd vertex. In this figure, beginning at an odd vertex means you will end at an odd vertex.

What happens if you start at *A* or *C*, which are even vertices? Try it and find out.

Surprise! It cannot be done. You always have at least one path you cannot trace. Two possible answers are shown, starting at *A*. This last experiment means some-

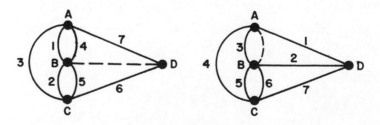

thing must be added to Euler's rule—the dotted lines cannot be drawn without breaking the rule. We have to start at an odd vertex to trace out the network completely. We cannot start at an even vertex.

The adding of this extra line connecting A to C is the same as adding a new bridge over the river in Koenigsberg. In the real city this is now a railroad bridge. So, if you start at B or D you can make the complete tracing.

There was also another new bridge built, so that a map of the city with its nine bridges looks something like the picture.

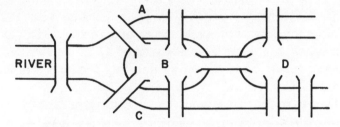

It too can be drawn as a network. The squares, again, rep-

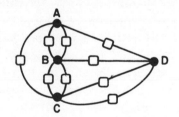

resent the bridges. There are still two odd vertices, B and C, so the tracing can be done, but only if you start at B or C. The diagrams show two possible ways.

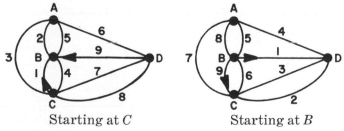

Starting at C Starting at B

21

(A)

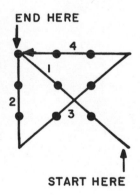

END HERE

4

1

2

3

START HERE

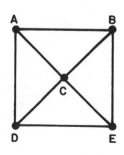

Again the same thing happens. If you start at an odd vertex, you end at the other odd vertex. If you start at *C*, you end at *B*, and vice versa. These types of figures where all the paths can be traced in a continuous line without crossing or retracing are called Eulerian (Oil-er-e-an) figures. They were named after Leonhard Euler, who first solved the problem. Topologists call such a solved and proved problem a *theorem* (thee-rem). A theorem is a law of mathematics.

The next problem concerns nine dots in rows (A). Copy them this same way on a sheet of paper. The problem is to draw four *straight* lines through all nine dots without lifting your pencil from the paper and without retracing any line. Lines may cross one another. The only hint is not to let your lines be confined by the square figure the dots form! Now you may think that the lines will look like the letter E.

There are four lines and they are straight. So far you have satisfied part of the directions for the problem, but you have not followed all directions! You had to remove your pencil from the paper to draw the middle line, or you had to retrace over some lines.

You must start thinking of drawing parts of the lines outside the square formed by the dots, thinking "topologically" about the problem. Form nine dots again and work on it for a while. The drawing shows the solution. We have only four straight lines, and they can be drawn without lifting the pencil from the paper. We did not retrace any line.

Let's try another network. It is a simple square with the opposite corners or vertices connected.

If you count the number of even vertices and the number of odd ones, you will see that four vertices have three lines meeting, so they are odd. Only one, *C*, joins an even number of lines. The problem cannot be done, because we can have only two odd vertices. If you don't believe it, try it!

There is always at least one line that you cannot trace. Four different ways to try are shown on the opposite page.

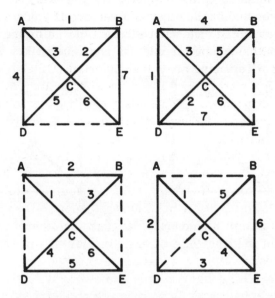

Again, the dotted lines are the ones you cannot trace. In the first two tracings, starting at *A* and going to another odd vertex leaves only one line that cannot be traced. In the second two tracings, starting at *C*, the only even vertex, and going to the odd vertex *A*, leaves *two* lines that cannot be traced. But there is something to notice here. Although you cannot trace all the paths, you have managed to touch all the vertices. This kind of path is called a *Hamiltonian* path, named after the Irish mathematician William Hamilton, who first studied such paths.

In order to make the network traceable, we have to create a figure with only two odd vertices. As you see, we can do this by connecting *A* and *D* with another line.

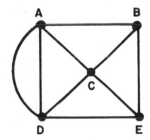

Now you should be able to trace the network, but *only* if you start at *B* or *E*, because these are the odd vertices. You will run into the same problem as before if you do not start at one of these odd vertices. Two ways to trace the network are drawn.

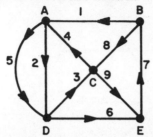
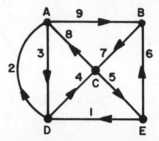

You can surely find more. You will discover that when you begin at either odd vertex, you will end at the other odd vertex.

So far, all our figures have had two odd vertices. Euler's rule says that a network can also be traced if there are *no* odd vertices. We have seen that a square (a figure with four sides) with opposite vertices cannot be traced. Let's try a five-sided figure with all the opposite vertices connected. This figure is called a *pentagon*, and the central star is call a *pentagram*. *Penta* means "five" in Greek, and the five-sided star is a common figure. If you count the number of vertices, you will find there are ten and all of them are even. Since there are no odd ones, the network (which is of degree four) can be traced. Try it without crossing any lines.

Two ways are pictured.

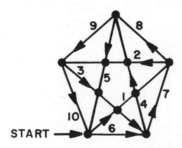
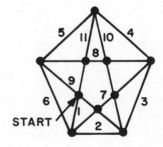

If another side is added, we can form a hexagon and can connect the center with all the vertices.

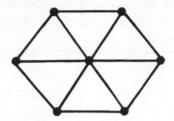

Is this network traceable? Before you try it, count the number of odd and even vertices. Six are odd, so it cannot be traced, whether you let the lines cross or not.

If you are still not convinced that just counting the odd vertices is the easiest way to find out if a network is traceable, go ahead and draw dozens of networks and try to trace them. You can prove to yourself that only two or no odd vertices can be allowed for a network to be traceable. It is a sort of "natural law" that Euler's formula for the dots, lines, and regions is related to the number 2, and that 2 is also the number of odd vertices needed in a traceable network. It is another invariant. As a quick problem, how many letters of the alphabet and how many numerals (0 to 9) are traceable?

Here is another type of problem like the last few.

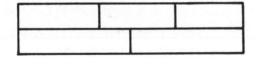

In this figure, try to cross all the lines just once without taking your pencil off the paper.

You will see that it cannot be done on a sheet of paper. Think for a minute of the same figure drawn on a sphere. Can you do it now? If you have a ball or globe, draw the figure and try again.

It still cannot be done. We will meet a figure later on, on which this problem can be done.

Networks that do not intersect are used in science. Let us take a look at printed circuits. These are used in radios, transistor radios, TV's, space satellites, and many other electronic inventions. They take the place of heavy wires that connect the various electrical parts together. The wires provide a path for the electricity to move through the instrument and make it work. If the wires cross or touch, a short circuit is made and the instrument stops working. So that this will not happen, we must get rid of all short circuits that might be made by accident. This is what the printed circuit is used for. Very small wires are built right into a piece of plastic in such a way that no short circuits are made. The problem is to connect the "built-in" wires so none cross or touch.

The pictures show three examples of such printed circuits before the wires are put in. The problem is to connect each pair of dots, A with A, B with B, and so on. Do this for each figure. The answers are in the back of the book.

Your lines in the last two problems must follow along the lines already drawn.

There are some interesting games dealing with networks. One is played with a dime and a penny. On the network in the square, place the penny on number 2 and the dime on number 4. The players are to take turns, making all moves along the lines. The penny moves first. The idea is for the penny to capture the dime by moving to the

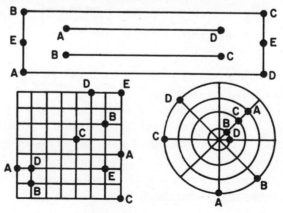

same point, but the penny must do this before he makes his seventh move. If he has made six moves and has not caught up to the dime, the penny loses. There is a simple way always to win. Can you figure it out? The answer is in the back of the book.

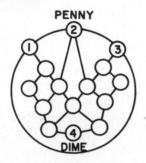

PENNY

DIME

The next game was invented in 1967 at Cambridge University in England by a mathematics student. It is called "Sprouts." The game begins with a certain number of dots. You make a move by drawing a line connecting one dot to another and then putting a new dot anywhere on the line you have drawn. There are two rules: First, the line may have any shape, but it cannot cross itself or any other line or pass through any dot. Secondly, only three lines can touch any one dot. The winner is the *last* person able to draw a line. Here is an example of a game of Sprouts with just two dots.

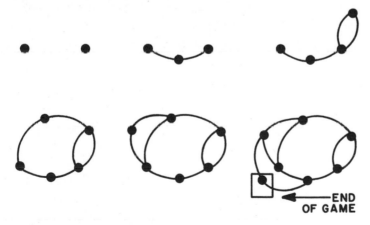

END OF GAME

ALL DOTS HAVE 3 LINES CONNECTING THEM.

Here is a game of Sprouts with three dots.

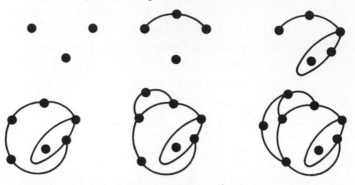

You can see this can get very complicated with four or more dots. Try it!

Another game like this is called "Brussels Sprouts." This game begins with a certain number of crosses instead of dots. The arms of the cross are where you start the lines. When you have drawn a line, you put a crossbar anywhere on that line. As with the game of Sprouts, no line can cross another or go through any cross. The winner is the *last* person able to draw a line.

Here is a game of Brussels Sprouts with two crosses.

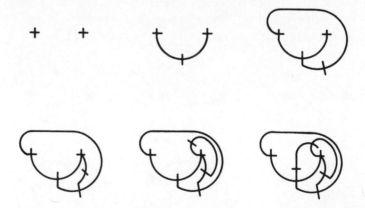

Play "Brussels Sprouts" with two and then three crosses. As you see, the networks we have explored look something like mazes—a good topic to start in our next chapter!

3

Mazes and Puzzles

In doing a maze, you may not take your pencil from the paper, cross any line in the figure, or cross the path you were drawing. To warm up to the idea of mazes, try some more networks. A maze is a network of a special type. Here is a simple type of maze.

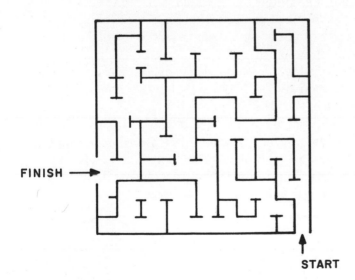

Our first *new* network is made up of three rings. Now you may have seen this network somewhere before, but it is really a very old symbol used by a very old Italian family. It is called the Borromean Rings. Copy the drawing.

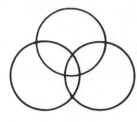

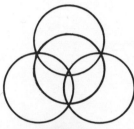

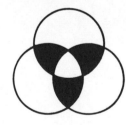

Or like this:

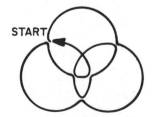

Now trace it so that no lines cross. In other words, make an Eulerian path. If you count the number of even and odd vertices, you will quickly see if it can be done. An answer is in the back of the book.

Try a maze with three squares. This one was invented by a very famous author of a very famous book, *Alice in Wonderland*. He was Lewis Carroll, and he liked to invent mathematical games.

Again copy the figure and try to trace it out without crossing any lines.

Now try tracing a third figure, made of four circles.

The answers to these puzzles can be made a lot easier by doing something to the figures that was thought of a few years ago by a mathematician named Thomas O'Beirne of England. He also invented the four-circle problem. He darkened *every other* region. The illustrations show two ways to do this.

Now O'Beirne says you can just go along the edges of these darker regions and find the path that doesn't cross. The drawings below show two ways to do this. The corners of the figures have been rounded to make it easier to see the final figure.

Now, you try the same thing on the three squares of Lewis Carroll and on Thomas O'Beirne's four rings. (Answers are in the back of the book.)

You might also want to see if you can trace these networks allowing lines to cross. The Borromean rings and O'Beirne rings are not very difficult, but Lewis Carroll's three squares need a bit of thought. If you do not start in the right place, you cannot trace them.

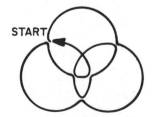

START

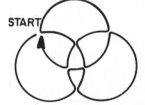

START

Now let's explore the subject of regions a bit further.

30

A circle drawn on a piece of paper divides the paper into two regions—one inside the circle and one outside. If we put a dot inside the circle and another outside the circle, you can see that any line connecting the two dots will cross the circle. Now, let's change the shape of the circle. Look at the series of pictures, which shows how we are going to do this.

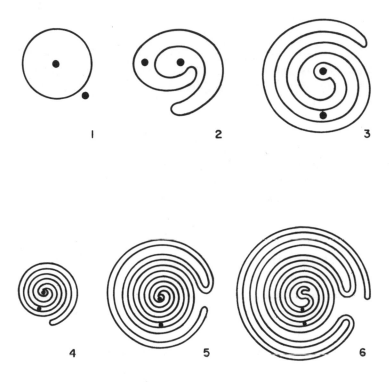

Note that we still have two dots. One is in one region and one is in the other. But can you tell which dot is where? Copy the last figure very carefully on a piece of paper and see if you can think of a way to discover which dot is inside the curve and which is outside. This is really not so difficult as it seems. Here is a hint. Use red or blue pencil to color the inside region. You will quickly find which dot is inside. It is the same as if you colored in the plain circle.

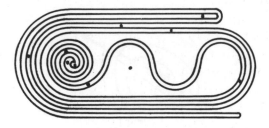

From these last simple experiments, you can see that all the figures have an inside and an outside, no matter how we twisted them. In topology, we say that the figures on page 31 are all "topologically equivalent." This means that all these figures are alike in that they have an inside and an outside separated by a Jordan curve. If we were to take a square and think of it as having sides like rubber, we could change its shape to a circle or an oval very easily. We'll return to this idea later.

One of the most famous of mazes comes from the island of Crete, in the Mediterranean Sea near Greece. One of the ancient rulers, King Minos, was said to have ordered built a large underground maze, which he called the Labyrinth. In the middle of it, according to the myth, was put a fierce monster, the Minotaur, half man, half bull. Now, the people of Athens, in Greece, were required by King Minos to send seven boys and seven girls as a sacrifice to the monster every few years. This went on for quite some time. At last, one year, a young man named Theseus came with a group of boys and girls. He carried a ball of thread with him. When the group was sent into the maze, Theseus unraveled his thread, found the monster, and killed him. He then rewound the thread and led everyone out of the maze.

Copying this labyrinth was a favorite exercise in the ancient world. Its form has been found on ancient coins and on the walls of houses. Children, especially, liked to see if they could copy it and then try to find their way in. Tracing the labyrinth is not difficult. Here are two forms of it, the square form and the round form. See if you can copy them and find your way in and out.

The thread that Theseus used was called the "Thread of Ariadne." In your maze it is just a pencil line. Now you will find that you will go through every part of the maze, leaving no path untraveled. Because this maze is constructed in this way, it is not really hard to go through. Drawing the maze is the hard part! There is a simple way to do this, but it took a bit of thinking.

Here is a diagram of the center part of the maze. All you have to do is connect all the numbers (1 with 1, 2 with 2, and so on) by connecting 1 with 1 the *long way* around the figure and cross *no* lines. Copy this figure near the top of a piece of paper and see if you can easily draw the maze. Start like this:

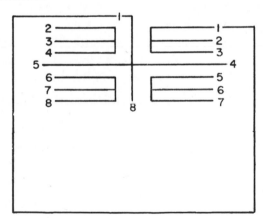

Then continue:

Next is a diagram for the circular form. Again, you must start by connecting 1 with 1 the *long way* around the figure and cross *no* lines.

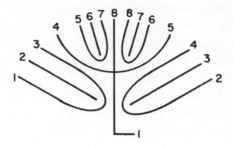

The real fun is drawing the maze, not going through it! Even though the shape of the two mazes is different, one square-shaped and one circular, you can see that they are topologically equivalent. In topology, we are concerned not so much with the shape of a figure as with the special properties it shows us. Both the mazes are constructed in the same way, except that one has square corners, the other round.

Another fact about the labyrinth we want to discover is whether it is a Jordan curve—that is, does it divide the paper into two parts? The only simple way to find out is to use a pencil and shade in the figure, starting from the inside. Do this to one of the labyrinths you have drawn and see if it is a Jordan curve. The answer and explanation are in the back of the book.

Mazes like these can be made a bit more complicated. You may want to make one with the next figure. Again, connect 1 with 1 the *long way* around the figure and give yourself enough room to complete it.

Is this maze a Jordan curve?

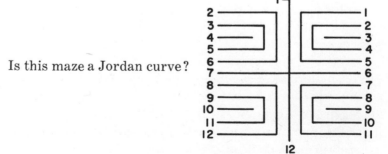

As we saw, these labyrinths are very easy to solve. Let's go to a more complicated type. Long ago a palace was built near London, England, called Hampton Court, which was famous for its gardens. The palace gardeners of that time (about 1520) created mazes out of hedges. Walls were also built in the form of mazes. You can see mazes in Williamsburg, Virginia, at the Governor's Mansion, that are copies of the gardens at Hampton Court.

Here is a diagram similar to the gardens.

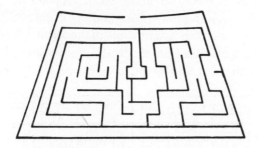

The goal is the space in the center. The problem is to think up a simple rule that will always get you there. If you just try any path, you will run into some blind alleys, but you can always turn around and continue. The idea is not to run into any of these blind alleys, but there is no rule to avoid them. One sure way of getting to the middle and out again is this rule: place a hand on any wall and then take no paths that require you to lift it from the wall. You will find that you will not cross all the paths. The parts of the maze that are not traveled are called "islands." Look in the back of the book for the solution and more explanation.

The next maze is more complicated. It was invented by a British mathematician named Dudney, who is well known for inventing many mathematics puzzles. The idea is to get to the dot near the middle. Try to apply the rule for the Hampton Court maze—keep one hand on any wall and take no paths that require you to remove it.

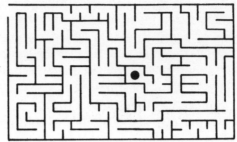

Can you do it? You will probably find that you cannot. Why? Because it has been designed in such a way that an island exists inside the maze that is disconnected from the rest. Here is the maze again, but just look at the dotted line that marks off this center island. You will see it is not connected to the rest of the maze.

ENTRANCE

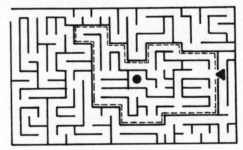

In order to solve this, you have to take your hand off the wall at least once in order to get to the inner part. Then you can finish the maze. This is a maze inside a maze.

4

Maps and More Networks

Maps fascinate a topologist, but his maps are not necessarily the kind you find in geography books. He likes to simplify things, so instead of calling the parts of a map the "states" or "countries," he just calls them "regions." Because they touch one another, he calls them "contiguous" (con-tig-u-us) regions.

The simplest map has two regions. There are two ways to make it. The first is just to draw a line across a piece of paper from edge to opposite edge, giving you two regions. The second way is to draw a Jordan curve on a piece of paper. Since the curve divides the paper into two regions, an inside and an outside, it is also a map.

Now the best way to see each region of the map is to color each a different color. Obviously you need only two colors for a map with two regions. You cannot use just one, for then you could not tell one region from the other.

Let's think of the next simplest map, one with two lines drawn across the piece of paper from edge to opposite edge and crossing each other. We have drawn them three ways. You can draw the lines any way to give *four* regions. All such figures are topologically equivalent. How many colors do you need to separate completely each region from the next? You might say you need four, but the answer is that you need only *two*. Why? That brings us to something else about the way a topologist thinks of map-coloring. The first of the figures is just a four-square checkerboard. Now you know that a checkerboard has

OR THIS:

OR THIS:

39

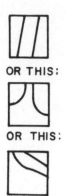

OR THIS:

OR THIS:

only two colors for its squares, usually red and black. And there is no confusion as to how the regions are separated. A topologist does not count the meeting of the four corners as really touching. Only the edges of the regions touch each other. So each of the figures needs only two colors, just as a checkerboard needs only two, or a tiled floor that looks like a gigantic checkerboard.

Another way we could make a map with just two lines is to draw them without letting them cross each other, as in these three examples. These patterns are all topologically equivalent. How many colors do we need for each of these maps? We still need only two colors, one for the middle region and one for the two end regions.

Still another way to make a map with just two lines is to let the lines cross more than once. You can let them cross each other twice, or three times.

Obviously we can keep on going, allowing the lines to cross many, many times.

The question is, how many colors are needed for these maps? Try to figure this one out before you look up the answer.

Instead of just two lines, we can use two Jordan curves to draw our maps, like the four shown here.

(One inside the other)   (Separated)   (Connected once)   (Connected twice)

Now these are not all topologically equivalent because of the way each is differently connected. But figure out how many colors are needed for each map. You should still find that you need only two in each case. Check your answer in the back of the book.

Now take a piece of paper and draw five lines, each con-

40

nected to the edge of the figure, and five Jordan curves to make a map. You make it by drawing the lines any way you want. Your map might look something like this one. How many colors are needed for the map? Still only *two!* Your map might look like a work of modern art, but don't try to sell it!

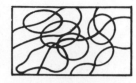

What you have discovered in the figures is the basis of what is called the "Two-Color Theorem." Do you remember what a theorem is? This Two-Color Theorem says that if you draw lines any way you wish or any Jordan curve anywhere you wish on the map, you will still need only two colors. Here is the last map colored in.
Let's draw a line across the map. The line can be any line, such as the one straight from one corner to the opposite corner, in the figure.
Now to see that we still need only two colors, all we have to do is to *reverse* all the colors below or above the line we have drawn. It will look like the next drawing.

Experiment with more complicated maps. If we have one like the round map, how many colors are needed to tell one region from another? (Black or white can be map colors.)

You can see that you need three colors. Let's add another region right in the middle of the figure.

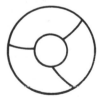

Now, how many colors do you need to tell one region from another? You can soon see that it must be four.

Well, let's keep adding more regions. We will add one as in the next round figure.

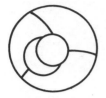

How many colors do you need? Five, right? *Wrong!* You will need only four! If you color it as indicated on the diagram,

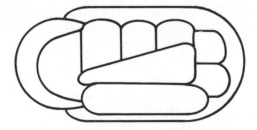

you see that only four are needed to tell one region from another! Of course you could use five, but you do not *have* to! Four are sufficient. This is the beginning of the very famous Four-Color Map Theorem of topology.

No matter how many regions in a map, only four colors are needed to tell one region from another. This surprising fact has been known by map makers for centuries. If you have an atlas in your home, look at the map of a state. You will see that only four colors have been used to separate the counties of the state. This makes the printing of the book cheaper.

Here is a very complicated map that looks as if it needs more than four colors to separate each region, but work on it for a while and you will discover that you still need only four colors. Check your answer with the solution in the back.

Probably you will not be able to get the right combination of colors the first time. But, there is an arrangement of just four colors that will separate one region from another. The solution is in the back of the book.

The most surprising thing about this Four-Color Theorem is that no mathematician has ever been able to prove it. By "proving" that something is true, a mathematician or scientist shows himself and everybody else, by mathematical logic, that it will *always* be true. The only reason a topologist believes this theorem is because it works when he does just what we have been doing. Let's see if we can find some reasons why it works.

We are going to start with four regions, as shown previously. You found that four colors are needed. Now by adding the fifth region, you can see that is it completely separated from the region at the top, and because it is completely separated we can color both 1 and 5 with the same color.

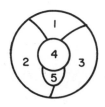

Now if we add another region, 6, we have separated region 3 from region 4 and can color these two with the same color.

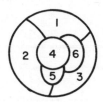

The best way to think of what happens when you add a region is this: If you add a small region, it will be completely separated from at least one other region and so can be colored the same as that region. If you add a large region, it is so large that it does not allow some regions to be adjoining neighbors any more. No matter how many regions we add, we need only four colors or less.

An old story about regions was first told by a German astronomer and mathematician named Ferdinand Moebius (Mer-bee-us). IIe was one of the founders of the study of topology. The story goes like this: There once was a man with five sons. When he died, his will said that his land was to be divided between his sons so that each would be a neighbor to the other. This meant that the land of any two of the brothers had to have at least *one* edge in common, and not at just one point. Each brother's land also had to be in one piece. See if you can figure out if this can be done.

To get on the right track, let's try an answer to the problem.

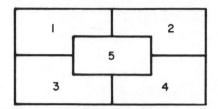

At first this looks like the answer. Can you see why not? Region 5 is a neighbor to all the rest, but region 1 is not a neighbor to 4 and region 2 is not a neighbor to 3. It is like the four-color map problem. Let's try another one.

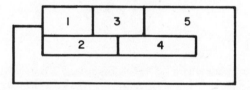

In the drawing do you see which two regions are not neighbors? (Regions 1 and 4.) You can try more solutions, but you will find that there will always be at least two regions that are *not* neighbors. No matter how you do it, two of the regions will *always* be separated!

An interesting extension of the study of maps is the construction of the "dual" of the map. A dual is a network that represents the map. If we take a map, put a dot in each of the regions, and then connect the dots with lines that correspond to borders in the original map, we have made a network that represents the map. Here is a sample of the three-region map.

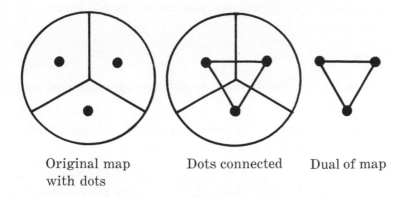

Original map   Dots connected   Dual of map
with dots

Here is one for the four-region map.

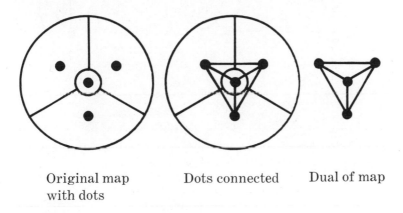

Original map   Dots connected   Dual of map
with dots

Now, instead of coloring the map, we can color the lines
of the dual so that no line touches another of the same
color. Here is a sample for the dual of the four regions.

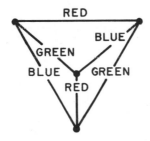

The dual for the three-color map needs three colors.

If we construct the dual of the five-region map, how many colors are needed to separate the lines?

Original map   Dots connected   Dual of map
with dots

This may be difficult, so the drawing gives the solution.
It takes five colors!

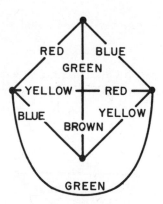

We can extend this idea of coloring the lines of net-works. You remember that the degree of a network is the number of lines meeting at a vertex. For example, this figure is of degree three, since there are three lines meeting at each vertex.

46

The coloring is called the Frontier Color Problem. The question is this: what is the smallest number of colors needed to separate the lines? Try the above network and see if you can find out. The number is three, and the explanation is in the back of the book.

The problem then says to add another line and two new vertices, as in the diagram.

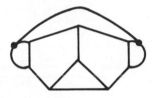

Now, can you still show that three colors are enough to separate each of the lines?

In fact, any network of degree three requires only three colors. Try these and see if it is true. Some are not so simple as they seem.

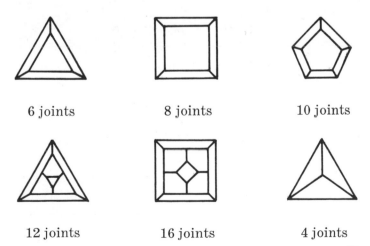

6 joints   8 joints   10 joints

12 joints   16 joints   4 joints

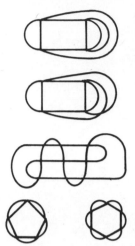

If we extend this idea of coloring networks to networks of degree four, can we still find a minimum number of colors? We might suspect that since networks of degree three require only three colors, maybe networks of degree four will require only four colors. Try these for a while and then see if you agree with the answers in the back of the book.

 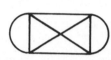 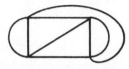

Now you have discovered that some of the networks of degree four could be colored with just four colors and some could not. Let's see why. Count the number of vertices in each of the degree-four networks. Do you find any relationship between the networks you could color and the number of vertices, odd or even, in the networks? Those networks with an even number of vertices can be colored with just four colors, but those with an odd number of vertices cannot.

You can keep on making networks of higher degree. Try some of degree five. This means that every dot has only five paths leading away from it.

Again, find out which ones need only five colors and then see if you agree with the answers in the back of the book.

You can draw other networks of degree three, degree four, and degree five. Try this and see if you can color them with the proper number of colors. In drawing the degree-three networks, you will find that they can always be colored with just three colors! Why? Count the number of vertices in each. You will see that it is always an even number. Just try to draw a network of degree three with an odd number of vertices. It cannot be done.

If you want a harder problem, try to draw a degree-five network with an odd number of vertices. This cannot be done either!

It is easy to see why these last two types of figures cannot be drawn. Just think of the vertices with paths coming from them. For example, here is the degree-three network with just three vertices.

Now if you connect all the paths, there is a place for a path left over that cannot be connected to anything.

Where to next?

The degree-five network with just three vertices will look something like this *before* the paths are connected.

Where to next?

Now if you try to connect all the paths, there is still one left over!

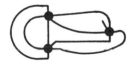

49

The reason is that the number of paths in each case is *odd*. If you try a degree-four network before you connect all the paths, you can see that the number of paths is always even.

All can thus be connected.

This reminds you of the game of "Sprouts" in Chapter 2, doesn't it?

5

Tiling and Reps

Let's explore the design on tiled floors, which is related to maps. We are not going to use actual tiles on floors, but we can draw them on paper. Do not get "floored" by some of the findings or "grounded" by discoveries!

Let us consider the idea of the floor. A topologist often thinks of a floor as part of a flat surface that never ends, which he calls a plane. A plane is a flat surface that is *infinite* and has no boundaries or edges. This may be a hard idea to think about, but mathematicians need to think this way. You can think of numbers like one, two, three, and so forth, going on forever. They never end. This is one basic property of counting numbers—they are infinite. A topologist just extends this idea to a plane.

Now to tile the infinite floor, which we are going to call a plane, we can use some figure that is of a certain size and shape and, if reproduced in great numbers, could fill up the plane. Let's take the simplest example—the square. Many tiles for floors are squares, and you know that a floor can be competely filled up with square tiles. If there are no walls or edges to the floor, we can also think of a plane as being completely covered by squares, leaving no empty spaces. A checkerboard is another example of using squares.

or

Let's try another simple figure, a circle. Could we use circles of the same size to completely fill up a plane? You can see that the answer is no. There are holes left that cannot be filled up with circles, as in these figures.

We would have to use figures that are *not* circles to fill in the holes.

What about triangles? Can any triangle be used as a shape for tiling a plane? Try an *equilateral* triangle. This has three equal sides and three equal angles. You can see that it can be done. Our plane will begin to look like this.

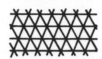

Now, how about any other kind of triangle? Here is an example. Could it be used as the shape to tile a plane? Trace and cut out many triangles like this and try fitting them together. Then see if you agree with the answer in the back of the book.

The only four-sided figure we have tried is the perfect square. Any kind of four-sided figure is called a quadrilateral (qua-dri-lat-er-al). Can *any* quadrilateral be used as the shape for tiling a plane? What about a rectangle? What about this figure? This is called a parallelogram. You can think of it as a lopsided rectangle. What about a trapezoid (trap-e-zoid)? In fact, what about *any* quadrilateral such as the next figure (it has no special name)?

The answer to these four questions is in the back of the book.

We have tried three-sided and four-sided figures. Let's try a five-sided figure, which is called a pentagon.

All the sides are equal in length, and all the angles are equal, so it is called a *regular* pentagon. We will use this term "regular" to mean all equal sides and all equal angles in a geometric figure. Now, back to the pentagon. Can it be used to tile a plane? See if you agree with the answer in the back of the book after you have tried it.

A regular six-sided figure is next. It is called a regular hexagon.

Can it be used to tile a plane? If it can be used, do you see why?

You can also try the regular septagon, which has seven sides, to see if it works.

The regular octagon has eight sides.

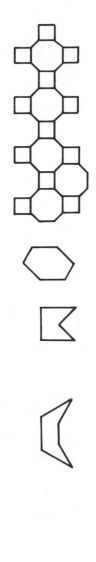

If you try to tile a plane with this figure, you will find you cannot do it with octagons alone, but need squares to finish it, as you can see.

You can try many more regular-sided figures, but you will find that there are *none* left that can tile a plane! You can use only triangles, certain quadrilaterals, or the regular hexagon. Let's go back to these figures and explore them further.

You have found that any shape of triangle, provided all pieces are the same shape and size, can be used to tile a plane. Regular quadrilaterals can also be used. The only six-sided figure we used was a regular hexagon. Suppose the hexagon is not regular. Can this figure be used to tile a plane? Try it and then see the answer in the back of the book.

So far, all the figures you have explored arc what we call *convex*. This means that all the sides bulge away from the center. To give you an example of a new type of figure, look at this pentagon. You see that two of the sides "cave inward." This is called a *concave* pentagon. It still has five sides, but is basically a different kind of figure. Can it be used to tile a plane? What about a concave hexagon?

Another type of experiment very much related to tiling floors is *polygon replication*. Here is an example to illustrate what this means. Using four equilateral triangles, can you connect them together to make a larger equilateral triangle? Four equilateral triangles make the big one. We say that the equilateral triangle can reproduce itself with just four smaller equilateral triangles. But, instead of saying all that, we can call it a "rep-4" polygon. This was the name given to such figures by Solomon Golomb in 1962.

to

53

Let's try any triangle.

Is this a rep-4? Trace the figure four times on a sheet of paper, cut them out, and see if they fit together to make the same shape you start with.

There are only two figures that are rep-2, that is, taking two of the identical shape to make a larger polygon of exactly the same shape. One is the parallelogram.

The second figure is a right triangle,

 and when put together with a second one, it looks like this:

Now let's try some rep-4 quadrilaterals. The perfect square is the simplest one.

A single one [square] will form a bigger square like this one.

Let's try a parallelogram with all equal sides, or a "rhombus." Is it a rep-4 rhombus?

In the next three experiments, carefully trace the figure four times on a piece of paper, then cut them out and fit them together like a jigsaw puzzle. These three trapezoids are the *only* rep-4 trapezoids.

Can you show that this is true?

This odd-shaped figure is the only rep-4 pentagon. Can you show how?

The next we have is a rep-4 hexagon; can you show how? You notice that these last two rep-4 polygons are concave.

So far, you have found that most polygons are rep-4. Let's see if we can find the next higher number rep by using equilateral triangles as in the drawing. You see that only equilateral triangles have been used and that our large figure is also an equilateral triangle. If you count the number of triangles, you will find nine. The triangle is thus rep-9.

Try this same idea with any triangle and see if it is also rep-9.

Now try the square, rhombus, the three trapezoids, the pentagon, and the hexagon that are rep-4. Are they all rep-9? The answers are all in the back of the book.

Tiling can also be done with curved figures. Here are different types of tiling that have been used in designs of floors and walls of ancient buildings.

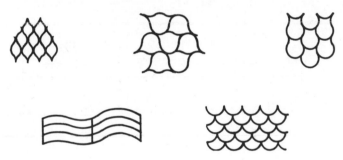

The last series of experiments in this chapter deals with equivalence classes and maps. If you have forgotten what an equivalence class is, check back to the first chapter.

Let's explore how many possible ways a circular region can be divided by a diameter of the circle and concentric circles. Concentric circles are circles that fit one inside another, all having the same center. The diagram is an example of three concentric circles.

If we begin with a single circle, we have one inside region separated from the outside. We called this a Jordan curve. We will label it "equivalence class 1." We explored this class on page 31.

55

Now, how many different ways can we divide a circle into *two* interior regions with just *one* diameter, or, *one* concentric circle? The diagram shows the only possible ways.

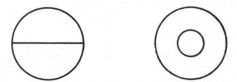

Now try the same idea with two diameters, two concentric circles, or one concentric circle and one diameter. You can see that there are only three possible equivalence classes.

You can proceed in this way, using concentric circles and diameters in any combination using four, five, and six lines. You can certainly go to higher numbers if you want to.

When you finish, you will find that the number of possible equivalence classes is always the same as the number of lines used, and it does not matter what combination of concentric circles and diameters you use! Always count the outside circle as one line.

You can also see that each is a map that needs only two colors.

Equivalence Class 4

Equivalence Class 5

Equivalence Class 6

6

The Surprising Moebius Band

The title of this chapter has nothing to do with music! The Moebius band is a strip of paper that is constructed in a special way. It was invented by the same Mr. Moebius we met in Chapter 4, on maps. You'll remember that he was an astronomer who was interested in geometry and who thought up problems in topology. The special paper band is his most famous problem.

To find out what is so special about the Moebius band, we have to check out some properties of a regular band. Get a strip of paper about six inches long and an inch wide and tape the ends together in a ring, as in the picture.

Now this band has two sides to it, just like the original piece of paper, and two edges. You can color one side red and the other side blue without any problem. If you cut down the middle all the way, as illustrated, what do you have when you finish? If you are not sure, try it.

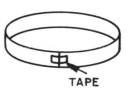

TAPE

You should get two bands that look the same and are similar to the original band, only just half as wide. They are topologically equivalent to each other and to the original band.

If you color one side of the regular band one color and the other side another color, you can very easily tell which side is which. All you have to do is to turn the band inside out. All two-sided figures are like this, and we call this property orientability (or-ee-en-ta-bil-i-ty). It means we can tell one side from the other.

We are now ready for the Moebius band. Take a paper strip ten inches long and an inch wide. Make a single twist in the paper, as in the drawing.

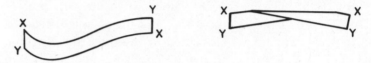

Now tape the ends together.

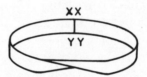

You have made your first Moebius band. Simple, isn't it? Now to find out how many colors are needed to color the sides. Just start to color the band at any place and see how far you can go before you have to use another color. Don't read any farther until you have tried this.

What happened? Only one color was needed! What does this mean? Well, if you used only one color to color the strip completely, the strip must have only one side! But you know it started with two sides. That is the important property of the Moebius band—it has only one side! Since there is only one side, try to turn the band inside out. It always appears the same, because there is no inside and no outside. There is just *one* side. You might say that its inside is its outside.

Try to find out how many edges the band has and you

will find another special property. The best way to follow an edge is to use a colored pencil and draw a line very close to the edge.

Keep drawing the line until you finally connect with the beginning of the line, where you started.

What do you find? The colored line had to be drawn only *once* along the edge, not twice as on a regular band. This means that the Moebius band has only *one* edge as well as just one side. It also means that the band is not orientable, because there is no way to tell one side from the other, since there is only one side!

Now let's see how the Moebius band can be cut. Cut down the middle as you did with the regular band and see what happens. The picture shows how to start.

Just keep cutting until you come back to where you started. Don't read any farther until you have done this.

More surprises! How many separate bands do you have? One? If you do not, you either twisted the paper strip wrong or cut it incorrectly. Someone was so surprised with this result that he wrote this rhyme:

A mathematician confided
That a Moebius strip is one-sided.
   You'll get quite a laugh
   If you cut it in half,
For it stays in one piece when divided.

No one knows the name of the poet who wrote this—he never signed it!

Now with your divided Moebius band, see how many sides it has and how many edges. Again, you will have to color the sides. When you have finished, see if you agree with the answer in the back of the book.

We now want to cut the band another way. It is sort of tricky, and you have to be careful. The band must be cut a third of the way in from the edge. The figure will help you to see how to do it.

This is very much like drawing a line close to the edge, except that now you are cutting it. Remember—only a third of the way in from the edge, not down the middle. Don't read any farther until you have finished. Do not cut crosswise at any point. Cut only straight ahead.

What happens? Of all things, you get two bands, and they are looped! And one is twice as long as the other. Now how many sides does each of these separate loops have? Again, color the sides of the figure and see if you agree with the answer in the solutions.

The next logical idea is to cut the Moebius band one quarter of the way from its edge. Try it.

Since the Moebius band has only one side, there are some network problems that can be done on it that we had trouble with in the first chapter. First, I have to tell you something about the lines on the band. A topologist thinks of a line on a side as being "in" the side. He thinks of it as being drawn with ink that soaked through to the other side. So, from now on, a line is "in" the band. Think of it as if the band were transparent, or as if it were made of clear plastic, so that the lines would show through.

We can think of a Moebius band without really making one, just by drawing a rectangle on paper and labeling it.

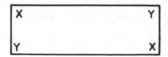

If the figure were cut out, you would make the band by putting corner *X* with corner *X* and corner *Y* with corner *Y*. Now draw a line down the middle the long way and label it *Z–Z*. Put one dot on each side of the line and label each. A dotted line from dot *D* to dot *P* will be drawn like this on the band. If the band were twisted and taped together, *P–D* would be one continuous line *in* the strip. Try it, using a felt-tipped marker that will show through the paper.

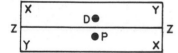 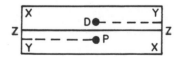

This idea is very important. A line that starts above the middle dividing line will end up below it, providing the line is "in" the band. This is what would happen if we made the Moebius band.

Now we can try some of those networks we were unable to do in the first chapters. The first one we could not do was the one with the five dots. If you remember, we wanted to connect each dot with every other dot without crossing any lines. We could connect only three of the dots to each other, as in the diagram.

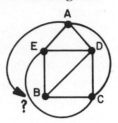

The only two dots that remain unconnected are labeled
A and *B*. You see we have to cross one line to connect
them, and this is not allowed. If you wanted to connect
them on paper, you would have to get the line mysteriously
from *A* to *B* around that line which connects *E* to *C*. If
you could make the line go above the paper like a bridge
over this line, you could do it. But that is not allowed.

The Moebius band allows us to do the problem. Here is
a diagram of the way it is done.

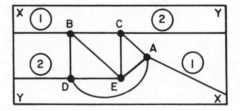

See how the line marked 1 starts from dot *A* around the
band to dot *B* on the other side of the figure? The line
marked 2 starts from dot *C* and gets to dot *D* around the
band. You have to remember that the lines are "in" the
paper.

The other network problem is the one with six dots. We
thought of it as three houses and three utilities. Each
house had to be connected to gas, electricity, and water
without any pipes crossing. One try is shown on p. 65, top.
You see we cannot connect house #2 with electricity without crossing some other pipe or line.

The Moebius band solves the problem. It is a hard one,
but it can be done. Try it for a while and then read on.

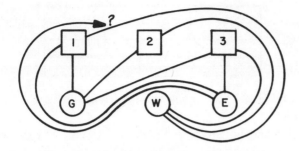

Don't lose your temper trying to solve the problem. It takes a lot of thinking. Here is the way to do it.

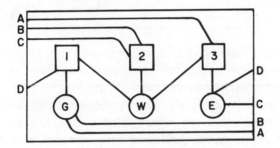

Now all the utility lines are connected to each house and none cross. Again, remember that the lines are "in" the paper and that a line starting at the bottom right, like line A, will end up at the top left.

We also tried thinking of the problem in another way: connect all the houses and utilities with separate telephone lines so that none cross. This means there are more lines to draw, but if you use the answer above, you should be able to do it. The solution is in the back of the book.

What about map-coloring on a Moebius band? Remember that the color is "in" the paper, showing on both sides. Try using typing paper and bright markers that will show through. To get you on your way in coloring such a map, here is one to color. Find out how many different colors are needed. The corners have been labeled because in a Moebius band opposite corners touch.

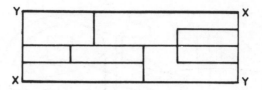

Try it and see if you agree with the answer in the back of the book.

Here is another map on a Moebius band. The directions are the same, and the answer is in the back of the book.

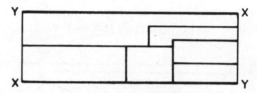

You have seen that a Moebius band has just one twist. You can explore the bands that have two, three, and more twists, or as many as you want to make. Try finding out the number of sides each has. Try also cutting these down the middle, a third of the way from the edge, and a fourth of the way from the edge. The answers for several of these are in the back of the book.

We are now going to explore a Moebius band of a special type. Make it with a piece of paper shaped the following way. Be sure you letter your band exactly the way the letters are put in the diagram.

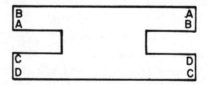

Twist the two tails of one end and connect A to A, B to B, C to C, and then D to D, like the pictures. Color the band to find out if it is one-sided. If you need only one color, then there is only one side.

There are several ways of cutting this band. You can start on one of the twisted sections and continue the same

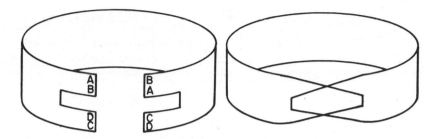

distance from the edge of the paper, as the picture shows.

You will find that you can do the same to the other twisted section and still have the whole band stay in one connected loop.

Make another of these double twisted bands, but this time cut it on a twisted section a third of the way in from the edge. This must be done very carefully and you may need some help in doing it.

Do the same to the other twisted section.

When you finish, you will have three bands looped together. Two of these will be Moebius bands and the biggest loop will be a regular band.

You may want to try to work with a band made from a big paper cross shaped as shown.

Of course, make your cross larger. Connect two of the opposite tails like a normal band and the remaining two like a Moebius band. Your band should look like the next picture.

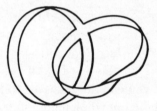

Now to find out how many sides this has, just start coloring and see how many colors you need to color it completely. If it is only one-sided, you will only need one color.

I hope you have found the Moebius band a lot of fun with all its strange properties. It has been used in statuary, for belts in machines so that they wear evenly, for tape recorders, for films, and even in some science-fiction stories.

7

Rubber Sheet Figures and Genus

So far, we have been exploring figures that are rigid and unstretchable. In the first chapter, we experimented with equivalence classes for the letters of the alphabet and for numbers. We said we could think of the letters as being made of rubber. This meant they could be bent or twisted but *not torn*. You can see how this works if you use a sheet of rubber or soft plastic. If you cannot find a sheet like this, you can cut a balloon and use it.

Draw the letter "I" on this piece of rubber. You can stretch and twist it to look like the other letters in the same equivalence class that we found in the first chapter. Remember, no tearing is allowed.

If you draw a square with a dot in the middle of it on this rubber sheet and then stretch it any way you wish, without tearing it, what happens? The square will no longer be a square, but the figure will still enclose a region. The dot will always remain inside this region, no matter how you stretch it.

If you draw a line from one corner to the opposite corner, there will be two regions inside the original square. Now, even if you stretch the rubber again, there will always be two regions inside the figure. We are not really interested in the shape of the region, but in the number of regions that remain after stretching. When the number of regions remains the same, we call the figure an invariant. Cut a hole in the rubber sheet. The hole is now like a region that is not connected to the sheet. Try stretching the

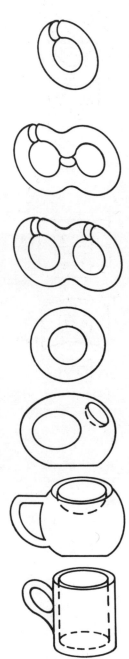

sheet and see how the hole still remains a single hole. It is an invariant.

Cut more holes in the sheet and then stretch it. No matter how you stretch it, the number of holes is still the same!

A topologist labels an object according to the number of holes it has. He calls a figure without holes a "genus zero" figure. If the object has one hole, it is a "genus one" figure, and so on. Another way to think of the genus of a figure is to find how many cuts are required to make it a single piece with no holes, a genus zero figure. For example, a doughnut is a genus-one figure. Now if you wanted to keep it in one piece, you would have to cut through the hole to make it genus zero. The picture shows the idea.

If there are two holes, it requires two cuts to remain in one piece.

Make some figures with modeling clay and try finding their genus numbers.

You can find objects of many types of genus around your home—buttons, pretzels, furniture, a piece of cheese!

The idea of genus permits us to classify objects topologically. For example, a doughnut is the same as a coffee cup. If you don't believe it, take your modeling clay and change a doughnut into a cup without adding any holes through the clay. You see that nothing has been cut or torn, only reshaped. No holes have been added or removed. The opening of the cup is not a hole—if it were, the coffee would leak out. Both figures, the doughnut and the cup, are topologically equivalent and are the same genus.

Can you show that a normal pretzel and a Halloween mask are the same genus? Both are genus three, so you should be able to distort one into the other without cuts or adding holes (first two drawings, p. 71).

Among the best examples of invariants are images in funny mirrors at amusement parks or science museums. You can find small mirrors of this type all around you. Look at your face in a belt buckle, a silver or polished metal bowl, a shiny lamp base or pipe, a curved store window.

In a flat reflecting surface you see yourself as you would in any mirror. But if the mirror is curved just right, your image will be reversed. Drawings A and B should help you understand.

The figure has been made with a square hole on the left side and a round hole on the right so that it is not symmetrical (having interchangeable sides). With the flat mirror, the square hole appears straight ahead in the mirror. With the curved mirror, the square hole appears on the opposite side. But in either case, there are still two holes, so the original figure and all reflections of it are invariant.

Your reflection is also invariant—you still have two eyes, and your nose is still in the center of your face. Different-shaped mirrors can be turned in different ways to produce different-shaped images, but all the images of your face are invariant.

In our first chapter, we talked of equivalence classes and grouped together letters of the alphabet and numbers with the same characteristics. They can also be grouped according to genus. How many genus types are there for the letters of the alphabet? How many for the numerals?

We found, for example, that the letter A and the letter R were members of the same equivalence class, but that the letter P was not. Do you remember why? The letters A and R have two tails each, while the P has only one. But, if you group the letters according to genus, all three letters have the same genus of one, because each has one hole. You can easily see that grouping according to genus will have many more members in each genus group, compared to the number of members in the equivalence classes.

Here is a list of the letters of the Greek alphabet. Group

ΑΒΓΔΕΖΗΘΚΛΜΝΞΟΠΡΣΤΥΦΧΨΩ
αβγδεζηθικλμνξοπρσςτυφχψω

these according to equivalence class and then according to genus.

Here are some letters from the Russian alphabet to group.

БДЖЗИЛЦШЪЭЮЯ

бджзилцчщьэюя

The answers to these problems are in the back of the book.

The cutting of surfaces, which was against the rules in earlier chapters, has in certain cases a very important meaning in topology. The first one to study cuts in surfaces from a topological view was Georgio Betti. The minimum number of times a network or surface can be cut so that it will remain in one piece and also have genus zero is called the "Betti" number of the surface. The Betti number is related to genus, but is not the same.

First, let's find the Betti numbers of some simple networks we have seen. For example, a circle, square, rectangle, or any polygon all have the same Betti number—one. It requires only one cut to make the figure genus zero while it stays in one piece. The Betti number appears to be an invariant. Let's see if this is true of more complicated networks.

Consider the Koenigsberg bridge network. Can you see that its genus is four? There are several ways you can cut this figure. The diagram shows one way. Do you think it is correct? No, it is not! The reason is that the network is no longer in one piece. It has been cut into two pieces, so we have not satisfied the requirements for finding the Betti number. What about the cuts in the next three drawings? In each picture the network is cut

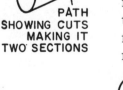

PATH
SHOWING CUTS
MAKING IT
TWO SECTIONS

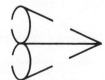
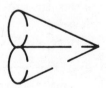

four times, yet remains in one piece. The Betti number seems to be four in each case.

Try to find the Betti number of each of these different networks (A–D). Check your answers in the back section.

The Betti number of a hollow sphere is quite a challenge. If you think about it for a moment, it is a genus zero, since there are no holes, and there is no place to start the cut. If you cut through a sphere, you end up with two half spheres—two pieces, instead of a single piece. If you put a hole in it, part of the original sphere is separated completely from the rest (E). So this surface, the hollow sphere, has a Betti number of zero. It points out the fact that a cut must be complete, not just partial. You could try cutting the sphere almost in half (F). Then you do have a single surface, but it is not complete and traceable as it was in the networks. Do you see that the Betti number for the hollow sphere with the single hole is zero?

Form some Moebius bands and cut them as before. While you are cutting these bands, you should discover what the Betti number of the Moebius band is.

Let's find the value for Euler's formula for networks on a Moebius band: the formula relates the number of regions R, the number of vertices V, and the number of edges E. We'll use the same form as before: $R + V - E = ?$ We can start with the simplified rectangle.

Without any lines at all on the Moebius band, what are the values in the formula? $R = 1$, $V = 0$, and $E = 1$. $1 + 0 - 1 = 0$. So the value is zero.

What about the regions on these Moebius bands? The regions are numbered to make the problem clearer.

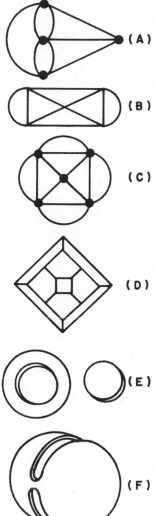

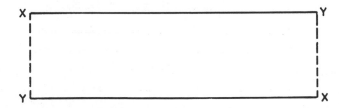

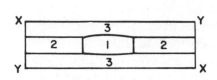 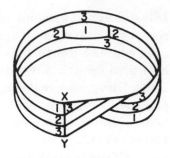

Here $R = 3$, $V = 4$, $E = 7$. So the value is still zero.

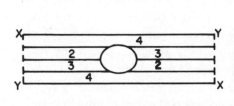 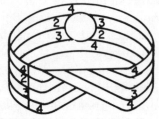

Now $R = 4$, $V = 6$, $E = 10$. Again the same answer.

Check these two figures, imagining them joined as twisted Moebius bands and see if you can make the formula still work, solving to zero.

Is a sheet of paper topologically equivalent to, and the same genus as, a hollow sphere with a hole in it? If we can form one into the other without tearing, adding holes, or subtracting them, the question must be answered yes.

Before we start, let's investigate the properties of each.

74

The sheet has two sides, one edge, and a Betti number of zero—you do not have to cut it because it already is in one piece and is a genus zero. The sphere has two sides, the hole is its edge, and we just saw that its Betti number is zero. Now what is the sphere's genus? You might say one, because it has one hole. But, this is not true! The hole is an edge, and does not go completely through the figure. It is a hole in a sense, but it is *not* a topological hole. So the sheet of paper and the sphere have the same properties. This means they indeed are topologically equivalent! How? Just follow the drawings and you will see.

If you look at the drawings in the reverse order, you see how the sphere is re-formed into the paper.

A most fascinating experiment dealing with genus properties of surfaces is the vest removal puzzle. If a man is wearing an unbuttoned vest with an unbuttoned jacket over it, he can remove the vest *without* removing the coat and without taking either arm out of the coat sleeve! You will probably say it seems impossible, but it has been known for a very long time that it *can* be done.

Now the vest is a genus-two surface—it has two holes for the man's arms. The jacket is also a genus-two surface, for the same reason. The vest is in no way connected to the jacket with any kind of knot—it is completely separate from the jacket. Really, both the jacket and the vest, and indeed any article of clothing, are completely separated from the man and from all other articles of clothing so long as none are knotted or hooked together. So it should be possible to remove the vest without removing the jacket. Use a loose vest if you can. Here are the steps in removing the vest:

Pull the left armhole of the vest forward and fold the left side of the coat back. Now put your left arm, coat sleeve and all, through the left armhole of the vest. Next slide the vest across your back, over the coat, and bring the right arm and coat sleeve through the left armhole of the vest. Pull the rest of the coat through the hole. Now both sides of the vest are on the right side, under the coat. All you have to do is stuff the vest down the right coat sleeve, and, presto! the vest is off.

The fact that this can be done means that the vest was never inside the jacket at all! Not topologically inside, that is.

Another old problem with an unbuttoned vest is simply this: Clasp your hands in front of you. Now, can you turn the vest you have on inside out without unclasping your hands? Try this for a while with a helper and then look for help in the back of the book. This can be done with a buttoned vest or sweater vest, but is a little more difficult.

8

Dots and Lines in the Air

Now that we have explored dots and lines on paper and rubber-sheet figures, we are going to see what happens when we can actually hold the lines and dots in our hands! How can we do this? Lines and dots on paper are not movable or stretchable. If we use strings as our lines and knots as our dots, we can. A loop will enclose a region, just as it does on paper, except that now we can twist the region and make different shapes. A string with one loop is a genus-one figure, two loops makes a genus-two figure.

Before we go farther, we must know something about knots in topology. Get some string and make a knot, following the drawing.

This is not a knot. Why? Because you can pull the ends and the knot can be undone. Try it. A topological knot is one that will stay a knot no matter how you pull it. For example, here is a knot.

The first experiment with a piece of string is one of the simplest. All it requires is a fifteen-inch length of string and yourself. The problem is this: Pick up the string by holding the ends of it in your hands and tie a knot in it without letting go of the ends of the string. The directions sound simple enough, but doing it is not so simple.

You have gone through all sorts of twisted-up shapes and not made a single knot, right? You probably picked up the string and held it as in the first picture. This is just what you are expected to do. But the directions did not say *how* to pick up the string. Perhaps you can think of another way of picking it up and tying the knot.

Had enough? There is really only one simple solution: before picking up the string, you should cross your arms in front of your chest. Now pick up the string at both ends, as in the figure. Now just unfold your arms and the knot will form. What you are really doing is knotting your arms. When you unfold them, you are transferring the knot to the string topologically.

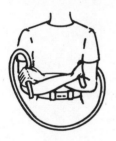

The next experiment with string and loops requires two strings that have a loop at each end. Make the strings about two feet long and the loops large enough to go easily over your wrists. You will need a partner to try this experiment. Place one of the genus-two strings on your wrists as in the drawing. Your partner should do the same with the other genus-two string, except that the strings must be crossed, like the picture.

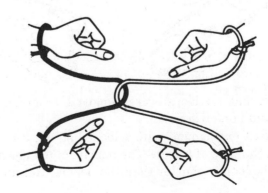

You see that you and your partner are looped together by the strings. The problem is to get apart without cutting the string or taking the loops off your wrists. You may both twist like pretzels trying to get unlooped, but you probably will not get untangled.

To get untangled topologically, you have to use one loop of your partner's string. Pull part of your string through one of your partner's loops,

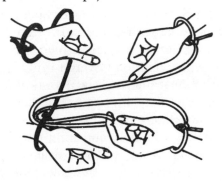

then over his fist,

then under his loop and off!

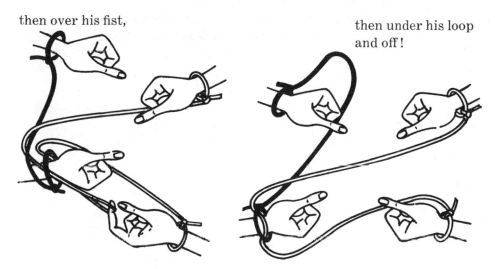

You see that no loops were removed from any of the wrists and none were cut.

The next experiment with a looped string uses a pencil and a buttonhole of a coat. The pencil simply has a loop on it, but the loop is shorter than the pencil. Get an old coat

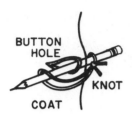

BUTTON HOLE

KNOT

COAT

that has buttonholes in it and put a pencil through a buttonhole, like this, tying to the eraser end a loop that is shorter than the pencil and goes around the point beyond the buttonhole.

The problem is to get the pencil and loop out of the buttonhole without tearing the coat or the loop or breaking the pencil, or sliding the knot from the pencil. Here are some hints.

Remember that the coat is not a rigid surface, but a bendable one. In other words, the part of the coat with the buttonhole can be bunched up to help you do the problem. Try this for a while, but don't overdo it.

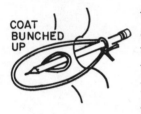

COAT BUNCHED UP

Give up? Well, here is the solution. Bunch the part of the coat with the buttonhole and pull it through the loop, as shown. Now try to pull the pencil backward through the buttonhole. As you keep bunching more and more of the coat through the loop, you will eventually be able to pull the pencil through the buttonhole, and the loop will just fall free.

If you want to show others this problem, start with the loop and pencil and work backward to get it in the buttonhole. Then ask someone else to remove it.

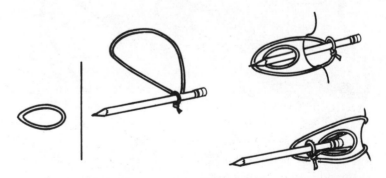

If you wish, you can bring the pencil all the way through the buttonhole and make the loop into a "knot." Be careful when trying to unloop it, because you must loosen the "knot" and remember to put the eraser end of the pencil first through the buttonhole. The knot is a real knot, be-

cause it cannot be undone by pulling further on its ends. To do so would rip the coat, and that is not allowed.

There are many other experiments dealing with knots and loops, some of them very complicated.

Next let's investigate the paper knot. The first question to think about: Is a paper knot a Moebius band?

To make a paper knot you need a band of paper about twelve inches long and half an inch wide. Tie the knot carefully.

Now, if you tape the ends without twisting them, is the knot a Moebius band?

You already know how to find out whether it is a Moebius band. The easiest way will probably be to draw a pencil line down the middle. If you come back to where you started and no part of the paper knot has not been traveled, the knot must be a Moebius band. Cut it down the middle. There is still a knot, but it appears double. Draw a pencil line down the middle of the cut piece and see if it too is a Moebius band. You've guessed that it is not. Remember what happened when a Moebius band was cut down the middle? It became a normal two-sided band with two twists. The same thing happens when the paper knot is cut down the middle.

Make another paper knot and try cutting it one third of

the way from the edge. Remember what happened to a Moebius band that was cut this way? See if the same thing happens with the knot.

So the paper knot shows several of the same properties as an ordinary Moebius band. There is one further property to investigate—orientability. Remember how we determined this property? We simply turned the band inside out. If we had a regular band, one side would be one color and the reverse side would be another. We could definitely distinguish one side from the other, so we said that a regular band was orientable. But since the Moebius band has only one side we cannot distinguish between "sides" by turning it inside out. Try the same test for the paper knot with its ends connected without twisting. It will help if you pull the knot so that it is somewhat tight as in the very last figure. I'm sure you will find that this paper knot is also not orientable, and so it shares this same property with the Moebius band.

You can also try a band that has two knots in it.

Does it show the same properties as the Moebius band? A single knot is like a single twist in the Moebius band, so two knots will probably be like two twists in the band. You remember that that was the same as a regular band without any twists—it had two separate sides and so was orientable.

The two-knotted surface is orientable because it has two sides, so if one side is colored red and the other green, you can turn it inside out and tell which side is which.

A very old topological knot trick is shown in the drawings on p. 83. Use a partner and a single piece of string, about eighteen inches long, with a knot tied at one end. The knot at the end is just to identify the ends. Tie up your partner's two index fingers following the drawings. The knotted end must *always* be in front of the unknotted

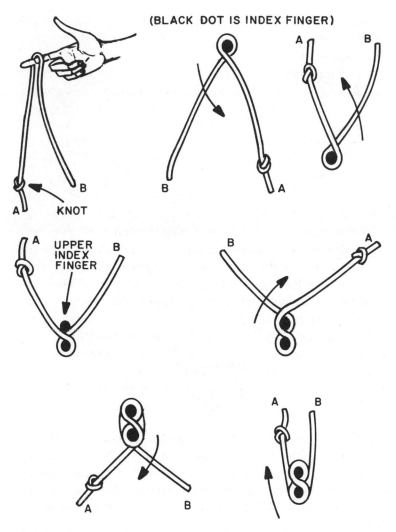

(BLACK DOT IS INDEX FINGER)

end in *all* parts of the exercise. Once you have your partner's index fingers tied up, ask him to remove the upper
one carefully. Then pull hard on the ends of the string.
To his amazement, the rope falls completely free of his
other index finger. You can tell him that the rope really
went through his finger! Of course he probably won't believe it. The explanation is that the "knot" is not really
wrapped around his lower finger, it just looks as though it
is. In reality, it is looped outside of his finger.

83

Another simple rope trick is the Chefalo knot. Start with a loose square knot,

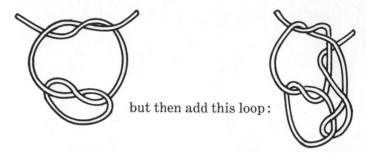

but then add this loop:

Make sure it looks just like the drawing. Now pull both ends quickly. Surprise! The rope has no knot at all. That extra loop eliminated it. You can do the same thing more slowly just to see where the square knot disappears. Without the added loop, the rope will knot.

One final experiment with a string loop is used with a buttoned vest. Ask the person with the vest to place his left hand in the *vest* pocket and then tie a loop made with a piece of string three feet long around the left arm. The other arm is *not* in any pocket. The problem is to get the loop completely off his body without cutting it or cutting the vest.

STRING LOOP

Remember that the vest is really not on the person at all, topologically speaking, and that you will probably have to use the fact that the vest has edges. The edges are the two armholes, the hole for the person's head, and the hole for his waist. Try this for a while on yourself if you have a vest or sleeveless sweater that fits you. Look in the back of the book for help.

9

Polyhedron Problems

In the other chapters we dealt with figures on a sheet of paper. In this chapter we will construct and investigate three-dimensional figures.

The first and most important group are the regular polyhedrons—you remember that the word "regular" means a figure with all equal sides and all equal angles. Polygons were drawn on a flat sheet of paper. Regular polyhedrons are three-dimensional figures with all equal sides, faces, and angles.

The ancient Greek philosopher Plato was the first to write about these figures, so far as we know. Later, people thought they were special and mysterious figures because there are only *five* possible regular polyhedrons. You will say to yourself, only five? You might think that from the many, many types of polygons you could certainly form almost as many polyhedrons.

To study these polyhedrons we must construct them. On the following pages are the plans for each. When you draw your own, be sure the sides of every polygon are equal. The dotted lines are where you are to glue or tape the figure together. The diagram with each of these plans will help you along. Each of the polyhedrons has a name.

A face of a polyhedron is any one of the flat parts and has the shape of a regular polygon. The points of the polyhedron where the corners of the faces meet are called "vertices," a word that you met in the first chapter. The edges of the polyhedron are where the "faces" meet. For

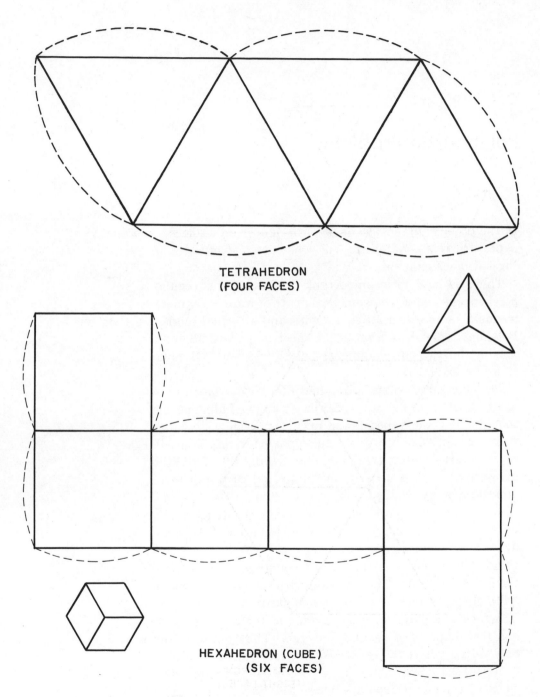

TETRAHEDRON
(FOUR FACES)

HEXAHEDRON (CUBE)
(SIX FACES)

86

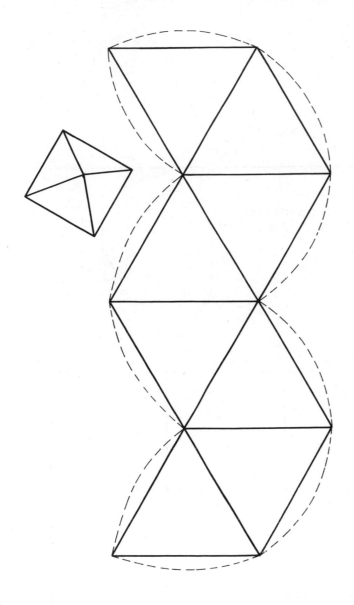

OCTAHEDRON
(EIGHT FACES)

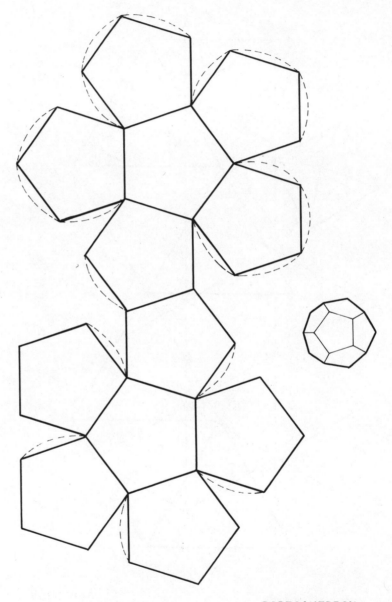

DODECAHEDRON
(TWELVE FACES)

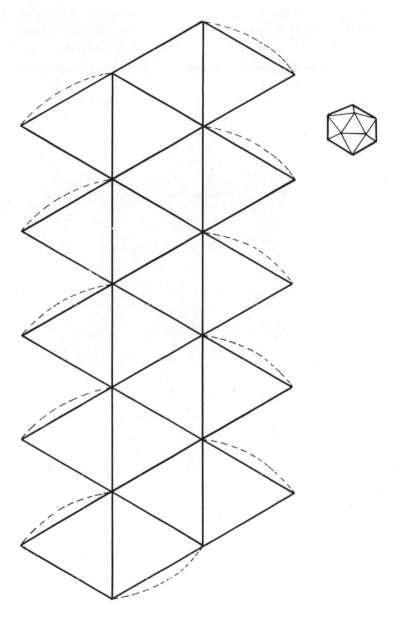

ICOSAHEDRON
(TWENTY FACES)

chapter.

Many, many more polyhedrons can be made if we do not restrict ourselves to a single polygon shape for each face. On the following pages are four more polyhedrons using several polygon shapes for faces. Trace them on a separate sheet of paper, cut them out, and fold as you did before. Try Euler's formula on each and see if it works.

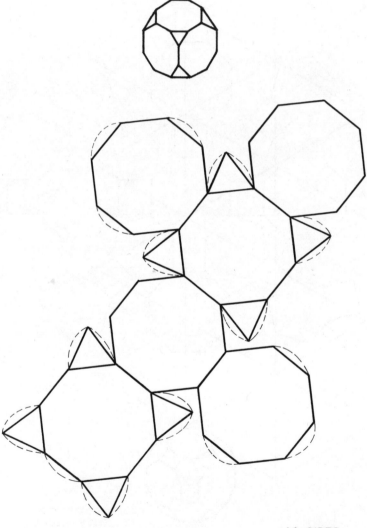

14 SIDES

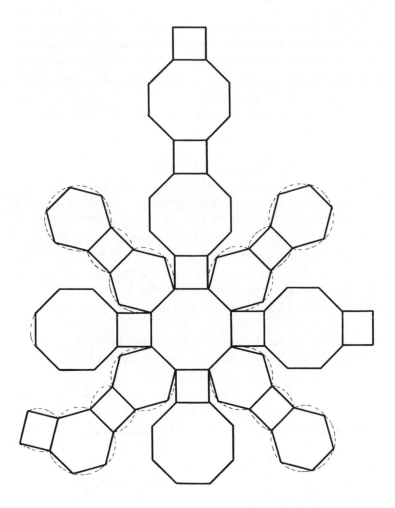

26 SIDES

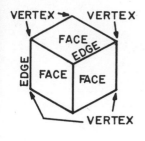

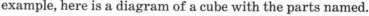

example, here is a diagram of a cube with the parts named.

Let's explore the faces of the regular polyhedrons as a group. You see that the equilateral triangle is used in three out of the five figures—the tetrahedron, the octahedron, and the icosahedron. The hexahedron, or cube, has squares for its faces. The dodecahedron has a regular pentagon for each of its faces. You can also see that at least three polygons meet at each vertex. The octahedron and icosahedron have more.

Let's check and see that only five regular polyhedrons can be made. Take a look at the tetrahedron. You see that only three triangles meet at each vertex. If we add another triangle to each vertex, we will end with the octahedron, with four triangles at each vertex. If we add still another triangle to each vertex, we will end with the icosahedron, with five triangles at each vertex. Now if we try to add still another triangle to the vertex, what happens? Take a look at the plan for the icosahedron on page 90. If we add that sixth triangle, we cannot fold the figure. In fact, all we do is to form a plane that is tiled with triangles! If we try to add a fourth square to each face of the cube, we end with a plane tiled with squares! So there is a limit to the number of figures we can use, and five triangles is the most we can have at one vertex, forming the icosahedron. We can have only three squares at each vertex, forming the cube; three pentagons, forming the dodecahedron. Four will not fit.

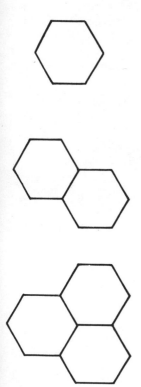

Let's see if we can form a regular polyhedron using polygons with more than five sides. We can try a hexagon, with six sides. We know that at least three polygons must meet at each vertex, so let's try to build up a plan to construct a polyhedron with just hexagons. We start with one hexagon. Then we add a second, and a third. Surprise! There is no space left to bend the edges, right? We are simply tiling a plane with hexagons and cannot possibly fold the edges.

If you try an octagon, with eight sides, or any polygon with more sides, you cannot fit three together at one vertex. Don't believe it, try it!

92

We can now explore the relationship between the edges, faces, and vertices. Here is a list of the numbers of these parts in each polyhedron:

	Faces	Vertices	Edges
Tetrahedron	4	4	6
Hexahedron	6	8	12
Octahedron	8	6	12
Dodecahedron	12	20	30
Icosahedron	20	12	30

Do you see a pattern in the numbers? There can only be 6, 12, or 30 edges in any figure. With the hexahedron and octahedron, the number of faces and vertices have been reversed; the same is true of the dodecahedron and icosahedron.

If we think of the faces as regions, the vertices as dots, and the edges as lines, we might be able to find a relationship between them as we did for lines and dots and regions in the first chapter. Remember what the formula was? Remember who discovered it? Will it apply to polyhedrons? Let's try it and see.

The famous formula discovered by Euler, the grandfather of topology, is: number of dots + number of regions − number of lines = ? To change it for polyhedrons: number of vertices + number of faces − number of edges = ? We are going to use symbols for these parts, so the formula will be written $V + F - E = ?$ ($V =$ number of vertices; $F =$ number of faces; $E =$ number of edges.) When you count the dots, regions, and lines in a *flat* figure, you get the answer 2. Maybe you should get a different number now, since we are not working with flat figures. Try it to see *before* you read any farther.

You still get the answer 2. You might think it should be something other than 2. But this is one of the great unifying ideas we gain from topology. It does not matter whether the figure is a flat one or a three-dimensional regular polyhedron, Euler's formula for networks still works! It is still an *invariant*, a word you met in the first

You have discovered that Euler's formula for networks also works for polyhedrons. This means that we can think of a polyhedron as a network that is not flat like a piece of paper, but takes up space.

Some networks, you remember, could be traced with Eulerian paths. This meant that all the lines and vertices were touched only once. There were also some networks that could not be traced; there was a line left that you could not trace although you could touch all the vertices. Do you remember what name we gave to a path of this kind? We called it a Hamiltonian path, after the Irish mathematician William Hamilton.

Let us find out if any of the polyhedrons you made can be traced with an Eulerian path or a Hamiltonian path. You can try this by tracing the edges of your polyhedrons with colored pencils. After you have tried them, see if your results agree with the answers in the back of the book.

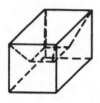

Now let's consider polyhedrons that are not convex like the ones you have made. The reverse of convex is concave. At the top of the page is an example of a concave polyhedron, where part of the figure caves inward.

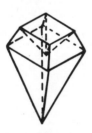

You see it is just a cube with a pyramid cut out of it. See if Euler's formula works: the number of vertices is 9, the number of faces is 9, and the number of edges is 16. Putting these numbers in the formula: $V + F - E = ?$, what number do you find? It is still 2!

Try the next four concave polyhedrons and see if the formula still works. Answers are in the back of book.

Now what about polyhedrons with holes in them? You might wonder if Euler's formula works for them. The bottom figure is a simple one—a cube with a square hole through it (a genus-one figure). When you count the number of faces, don't forget to include those that form the inside of the hole. You see there are four there. Now just use the formula. What answer do you find? It is still 2. Following are more polyhedrons with holes. Do the same and find if the formula works for all of them.

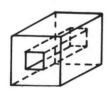

Can you see why the formula works for polyhedrons with holes like these? Let's go back to the first figure with the hole. Without the hole, it is just a cube with 8 vertices, 6 faces, and 12 edges. What does the square hole contribute to the figure? It also has 8 vertices, 12 edges, but only 4 faces. So in the formula the number of vertices is doubled to 16 and the number of edges is doubled to 24, but the number of faces is not doubled—instead it is 2 *less* than the doubled number of faces, or 10. So the formula will always equal 2. This holds true for any polyhedron with a hole that has *straight* edges.

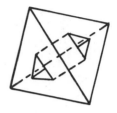

Well, what about a *circular* hole? Let's see if the formula works for a cube with a hole through it. There are 8 vertices on the corners of the cube, but the hole has no vertices, so the total is 8. There are 6 faces on the cube, but only 1 for the hole and it is curved, so the total is 7. There are 12 edges on the cube and two edges on the hole, but these are curved, so the total is 14. Using these numbers in the formula $V + F - E = ?$, you find that the answer is 1 and not 2.

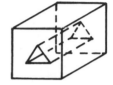

The reason for this is the shape of the hole. You see, a circular hole is not a polyhedron. Euler's formula works only for polyhedrons and other figures that have holes shaped like polyhedrons.

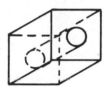

The coloring of polyhedrons is easy. The main problem is to find the minimum number of colors required. For the tetrahedron, you can easily see that four colors is the least, because each side shares one edge with another. What about the hexahedron (cube)? It has opposite sides that have no edges in common, so both can be the same color. There are three sets, so only three colors are required. The octahedron can be done in different ways, but there is one way to use a minimum number of colors (two). Try it and then see if you agree with the answer in the back of the book.

The two regular polyhedrons with the most sides, the dodecahedron and the icosahedron, are probably the most difficult to color. To make this problem easier, we are going to do something to the polyhedrons. We are going to

imagine that we can flatten them out, without tearing any
sides. In other words, pretend that they are stretchable
figures. Look at the pictures, flattening the dodecahedron:

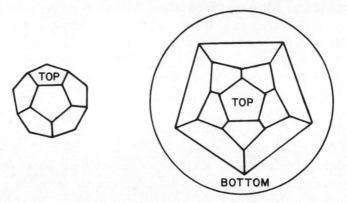

You see that the bottom face has become the outer bound-
ary of the flattened figure. It should now be easier to see
how you can color the faces of the flattened dodecahedron.
What is the minimum number of colors required?

The illustration shows what happens to the icosahedron.

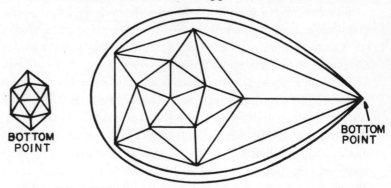

Use your imagination to understand this topological flattening. Although the sides are no longer regular polygons,
they are topologically equivalent to them. Work on these
for a while and then go to the back of the book for help.
One hint is this: such flattenings are really just maps.
You do know something about maps. Try this same exercise for the other two polyhedrons for which you were
given plans.

10

The Torus—No Edges

The next topological figure we are going to explore is one that has two sides but no edges. It is called a *torus* and is shaped like a doughnut that is hollow. You could also say that it is like an inflated tube used for bicycle or automobile tires.

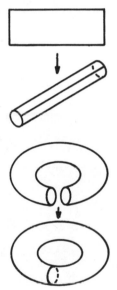

Since there is one hole in the torus, it is a genus-one figure. And since it is hollow, it must have an inside and an outside, a total of two sides. It is an orientable surface, for one side can be distinguished from the other, and there are no edges at all.

There are two ways to think of making a torus. The first is to take a piece of paper (or, which would be much easier, a rubber or plastic sheet) and roll it into a cylinder. Then you just connect the open ends.

The second way of making a torus is to take a short cylinder and connect the ends through itself.

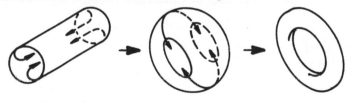

You see that both of these toruses are made differently. In the first one, the connection is through the hole. In the second one it is around the hole.

Let's explore the surface of the torus. Remember some of the network problems that you could not do in the first chapter? You discovered that some, like the six-dots problem, could be done on the Moebius band. You may suspect that since that problem could be done on the single-sided Moebius band, it might also be solvable on the torus. Before we explore it, try to do it.

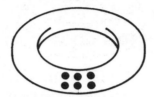

Here is part of one solution.

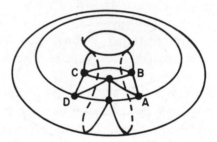

So you have to discover how to connect point A to point C and to connect point B to point D. There are several ways to do it, which you'll find in the back of the book.

Here is the second network problem that we could not do.

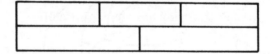

The object is to cross each of the straight line segments only once in a continuous trip. We found it could not be done on a flat sheet of paper, nor can it be done on the Moebius band. I wonder if it can be done on the torus? Let's see.

First, we will just draw the figure on the torus (p. 101, top).

Trying to follow directions, take advantage of the hole in the torus. Don't work on it too long.

You will find that it cannot be done. Why? Well, since

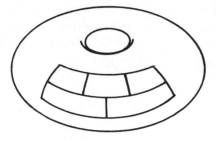

you are on one of the sides of the torus, the problem is much the same as if it were on a piece of paper. Let's try to position the figure a bit differently on the torus, as the figure shows.

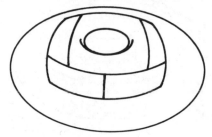

Now you may say that this is sort of cheating. But the figure is on the torus and we have only taken advantage of the hole. Now we could also turn the figure and position it another way.

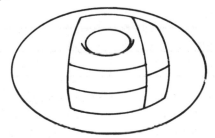

Try both of these and see if you agree with the answers in the back of the book.

What about coloring maps on a torus? What is the minimum number of colors required to separate all regions? You remember that the map-coloring problem is mainly one of neighboring regions. On a flat sheet of paper, only four regions could be neighbors. On a Moebius band six regions could be neighbors. Let's see if we can discover the greatest number of regions that can be neighbors on a torus. This is exactly the same problem as finding the minimum number of colors.

Obviously we can start with four regions that are neighbors.

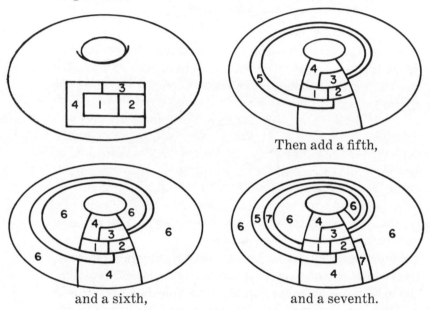

Then add a fifth,

and a sixth,   and a seventh.

Carefully check this figure (remembering that the torus has been flattened out) to see that every region is indeed a neighbor to all the rest. We are still all right, so see if you can add an eighth region. Notice that sections numbered 4 and 7 are really continuous around the torus.

Your figure probably looks very complicated. Well, it is complicated. You cannot add an eighth region. Seven is the greatest number of regions that can be neighbors on a torus. It is also the minimum number of colors required to color the map. You can have many more regions than the seven we have, but you will find that you will need, at most, seven colors to color the regions separately.

Here is one you can try. Remember that the torus is like a doughnut, so that some of the regions go around the hole and some go through it. This is why the regions are numbered. The solution is in the back of the book.

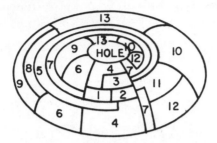

One of the most intriguing experiments with the torus deals with its orientability, since it does have two distinct sides. Orientable surfaces could be turned inside out, but how can we turn the torus inside out? Well, when you did turn some of the figures of the previous chapters inside out, they all had one property in common. Can you figure out what it is? Recall the regular paper band—it had two sides and was orientable. So was the band with two twists. So was the band with the two knots. You remember that the Moebius band was not.

The other common property, besides having two distinct sides, is the fact that the two-sided surfaces have edges. The figures that were orientable had two edges, and the Moebius band had only one edge. Well, back to the torus. It has no edges, right? So, if we want to turn it inside out, we will have to make some edges. We will first make one edge. How would you do it? You must remember that the basic properties of the torus must not be destroyed in making this edge. The torus must still have two sides and have a hole in the middle. Think about it for a while.

The only way to make an edge is to make a hole in the torus, as in the picture.

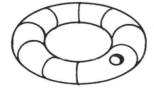

You see that the basic properties of the torus have not been destroyed.

We are now ready to see how the torus can be turned inside out. Look at the drawing to see how this will be done.

First cut or stretch the hole wider.

Then bend and start to pull the inside until it looks
the torus, to the outside, like this.

Now there is still a torus. All we have to do is to shrink the hole back to its original size,

   and then flatten the torus
a bit.

You see that the lines that were on the outside of the surfaces are no longer there. They have been transferred to the inside of the torus.

You can try to do this with a long rubber balloon. When you finish, it will look like the next-to-the-last figure, since you cannot flatten it as in the last drawing. Using a balloon is tricky, but you can do it if you are careful. Find a skinny balloon,

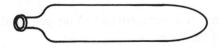

then cut the ends,

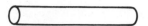

and tape.
(Two pieces of
tape, one inside and one
outside, will be stronger and less sticky.)

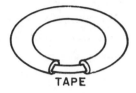

TAPE

You see that the enlarged hole is at the connection of the ends of the balloon. Your balloon torus will not look as convincing as the drawings do. The best thing to use would be an old inner tube from an automobile or an old bicycle tire, if you can get one. A torus made of paper does not work well at all.

You remember that a map is made up of regions. Now let's think of the regions on the torus and find out if there is a relationship between the number of regions, the number of vertices, and the number of edges, just as we did for networks. Our formula will be $R + V - E = ?$

We will first try the simplest map of a torus—a plain, unmarked torus. We will consider only its outside. There is but one region and no vertices or edges. So the formula equals 1.

Now let's put another region on it, say a square. So $R = 2$, $V = 4$, and $E = 4$. So the value of the formula is 2, just as it was for a network.

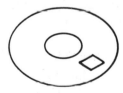
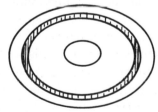

We now will put another region on it, but around the hole. So $R = 2$, $V = 0$, and $E = 2$. The formula has the value of zero.

What about the next torus? You see that the region goes through the hole.

103

goes through the hole.

What have you found? The formula still has the value of zero, right? It is the same value that you found for the Moebius band.

Figure out what value the formula has for the three map toruses. The regions have been numbered so that they are easier to see.

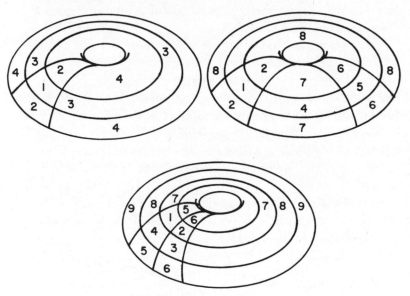

Let's see what the Betti number for the torus is. You remember that the Betti number is the minimum number of cuts required to make the surface a genus zero and still remain in one piece. Well, if you cut straight through it, you still have the hole.

So you must cut it again, lengthwise, to make it genus zero.

So the Betti number is two. Now we are right back to a figure similar to the one at the beginning of the chapter.

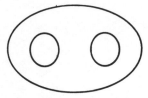

What would be the Betti number of a double torus, of genus two?

This takes some thought. You will end with several parts if it is not done correctly. Try it for a while and then read on. The pictures show that there are two ways to cut the surface.

You see that the Betti number is four, twice that for a

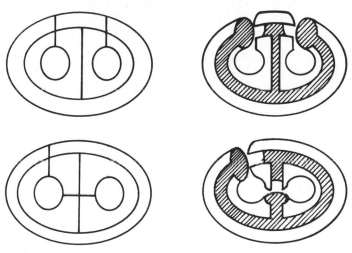

single torus.

Try this triple torus. You might guess that the Betti number will be six. Try it, then check the back of the book.

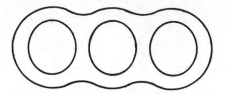

11

The Mysterious Klein Bottle

Another great German mathematician, Felix Klein, also worked with topology. He invented what he called a "bottle" whose inside is its outside. But neither he nor anyone else has ever actually made one. It is a topological bottle that can exist only in imagination. We can only make models that look something like a Klein bottle.

Klein started with a horn shape.

He thought of putting the smaller part of the tube inside the wider part,

and then cementing the edges of the open ends together, forming the opening, like the picture.

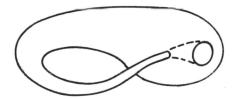

Now in real life, you would have to put a hole in the side of the original tube in order to connect it. But putting holes in figures is not allowed. You have to imagine that the connection can be made without a hole.

If you want to see what this looks like, you will need a balloon. Your balloon must be shaped something like the one drawn, with a long neck.

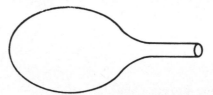

You now have to cut two holes in it. (Because you have to cut holes in the figure, it is not really topological, for cutting of surfaces is not allowed.)

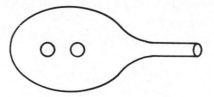

Fit the neck of the balloon into the larger part, pull it through, and connect the edges of the tube to the edges of the other hole. Now, where does the outside of the "bottle" end and the inside begin?

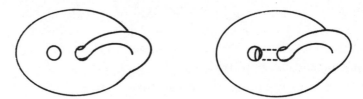

This is your first model for the Klein bottle, but remember, it is *only* a model. It is not a real Klein bottle, because of the holes in the figure.

The second model for the Klein bottle deals with two Moebius bands. A limerick will help you to think how we will construct it:

A mathematician named Klein
Thought the Moebius band was divine.
  Said he, "If you glue
  The edges of two
You'll get a weird bottle like mine."

Now a Klein bottle has no edges, but a Moebius band has one. So in order to make such a bottle from two bands, we will have to tape the edges of the two bands together. Let's see if this can be done. First of all, the Moebius bands have to be the same length and mirror images of each other.

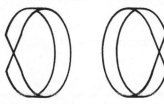

You now put a fold in each of the bands and place them together.

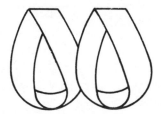

Now try to tape them together. You only tape the edges, not the fold of each band. The fold is the opening of the bottle. Your model should look something like the figure, except that it cannot be finished.

It certainly is terribly mixed up! You see that you cannot tape part of the bottle together unless you do some cutting of the bands. This is not permitted, but in the topologist's imagination the connection can be made without cutting.

Now, believe it or not, we can also make a Klein bottle from a single Moebius band. If it took two bands before, how can we possibly make the same thing with just one? The reason will be explored later. You will need a Moebius band shaped like this, only larger.

It can be made from paper, but rubber or heavy vinyl is probably the best.

This band must be carefully bent and taped in the right way. The diagrams show how this can be done. You will probably need some help doing it.

Ends taped together

Cutouts are for the neck of the bottle

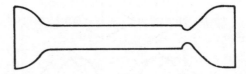

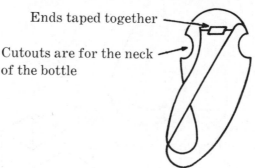

Completed bottle

Sides are folded around the neck of the bottle

Here is the reason why a Klein bottle can be made from just one or two Moebius bands: If we were to start with a real Klein bottle, we could cut it in several different ways —from which we would get a single band, two bands, or a pile of garbage. You have to know just how and where to cut it so you do not get a pile of garbage.

The last model for the Klein bottle will be the most ambitious. It looks similar to a stove.

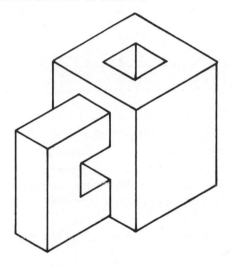

You can make this model in two parts.

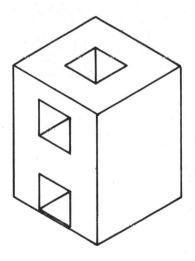
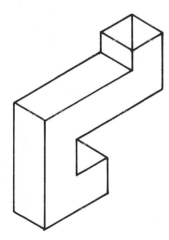

The smaller bent tube is then fitted into the larger box with the three square holes. We have given the plans for each of these parts. It is best to make them out of heavy construction paper.

Now can you tell where the outside ends and the inside begins? This is the mystery of the Klein bottle. It has only one side, like the Moebius band.

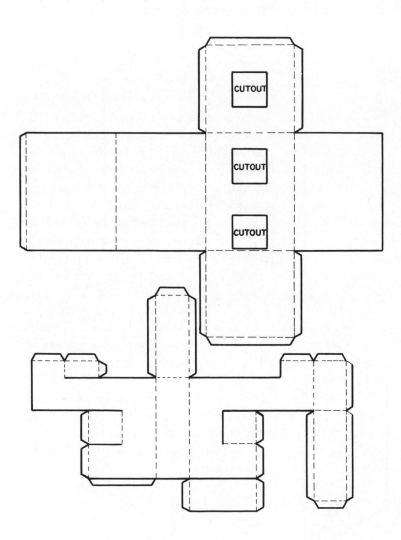

This Is Not the End

We have traveled from dots and lines through planes and solids to surfaces and new figures. We have dug a bit through some of the easier parts of the very large subject of topology. But the real digging is yet to come. There is still a lot to explore in the wonderful world of topology.

Sometimes the ideas that topologists discover cannot be pictured or simply explained like the experiments in this book. Often the only tools he has to experiment with are equations. Working with these tools requires a wide knowledge of algebra and geometry. Many mathematicians believe that topology will lead to yet undiscovered branches of mathematics. It is such a large and varied subject that this is bound to happen. Going deeper into the subject can mean doing without pictures and simple explanations. Some people can do this and some cannot. To people who study and use topology extensively, it is a very complex subject.

Whether you decide to explore further or not, I hope this book has given you a fascination for lines and dots and figures, and excitement for new mathematical ideas, and a feeling that you have found out something about the uncommon subject of topology.

Solutions

1. DOTS AND LINES ON PAPER

Equivalence classes for capital letters:

AR	KX
B	P
CLMNSUVWZIJ	Q
DO	Q
EF	R
GJT	
HI	

Notice that several letters can be written different ways, like

R and R , but each version is in a different equivalence class.

Equivalence classes for small letters:

aebdgpq	k
clsuvwz	hnry
ftx	o
ij	m

Equivalence classes for numerals:

12357	69
4	8
4	0

2. THE KOENIGSBERG BRIDGES AND NETWORKS

Capital letters that are traceable:

B C L M N S U V W Z D O P R

Numerals that are traceable: all but the numeral four written this way:

4

Networks in printed circuits:

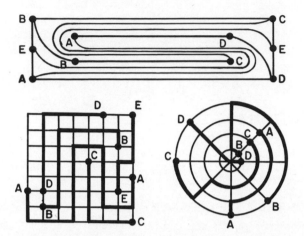

Penny and dime network game: You will notice that the three dots at the top of the figure are numbered 1, 2, and 3, and that the dime's dot is numbered 4. The best move for the penny is to go first to 1 and then, on the second move, to go to 3, but around the *outer* path. From here on, the penny will always be able to capture the dime on the seventh move or less.

3. MAZES AND PUZZLES

Eulerian path for the Borromean Rings:

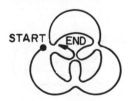

Eulerian path for Lewis Carroll's three squares:

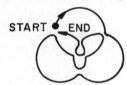

Eulerian path for four circles:

116

Jordan curve with ten dots:

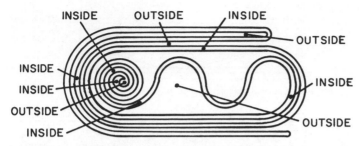

INSIDE OUTSIDE INSIDE OUTSIDE INSIDE INSIDE INSIDE OUTSIDE OUTSIDE INSIDE

Is the labyrinth a Jordan curve?

You can easily see that a labyrinth is *not* a Jordan curve if you shade it in. No unshaded regions will remain.

Williamsburg garden maze: The center of the maze is safely reached by placing the *left* hand on the wall of the maze and following that wall without removing your hand. Of course, you

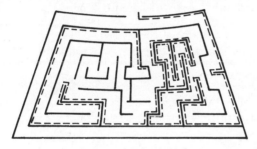

can reach the center without doing this, taking a shorter path. But in the real gardens, this did not work, because you could not see the whole maze at once.

4. MAPS AND MORE NETWORKS

Maps with only two lines connected to the edge of the figure: You need only two colors for each of these maps.

Maps with two Jordan curves: Again, only two colors are required for each.

Complicated map solution: The number in each region represents a color.

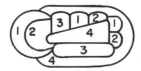

(Frontier Color Problem) Coloring of network of degree three solution: Each number represents a color.

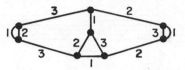

Coloring of some networks of degree three:

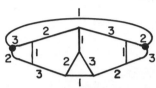 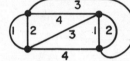 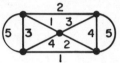 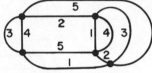

Coloring of some networks of degree four:

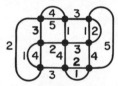 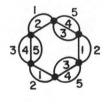

5 JOINTS (5 COLORS) 4 JOINTS (4 COLORS) 5 JOINTS (5 COLORS)

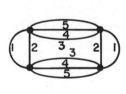 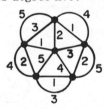

9 JOINTS (5 COLORS) 6 JOINTS (4 COLORS)

Coloring networks of degree five:

  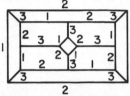

4 JOINTS (5 COLORS) 6 JOINTS (5 COLORS) 6 JOINTS (5 COLORS)

5. TILING AND REPS

Tiling with any triangle: Any kind of triangle can be used to tile a plane:

TRIANGLE:

TILED PLANE:

Tiling a plane with a trapezoid: Any trapezoid can also tile a plane, because the shape can be thought of as a parallelogram with a triangle attached to it, like this:

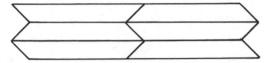

Either a parallelogram or a triangle can be used to tile a plane, so you might think that both together could be used. The trapezoid proves they can:

Can *any* quadrilateral be used to tile a plane? Experimenting will show you that the answer is no. This is true of the figure given:

Another similarly shaped quadrilateral will not fit into the empty regions.

Can a regular pentagon be used to tile a plane? Again the answer is no, as this drawing shows:

Can the regular hexagon tile a plane? The answer is yes, because the regular hexagon is made up of six equilateral triangles, like this:

Any triangle can tile a plane, so the plane tiled with regular hexagons is really the same as if it were tiled with equilateral triangles: This is the structure bees use in building honeycombs.

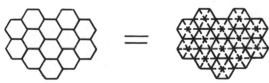

Can a tilted hexagon tile a plane? The figure given can be used to tile a plane: But *not* all kinds of hexagons can be used, because the same problem arises as with any quadrilateral.

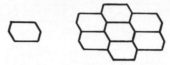

Can the concave pentagon or concave hexagon tile a plane? Neither of the two figures given can tile a plane.

The rep-4 triangle: *Any* triangle is rep-4:

The rep-4 trapezoids solution:

The only rep-4 pentagon solution:

This figure can also be used to tile a plane:

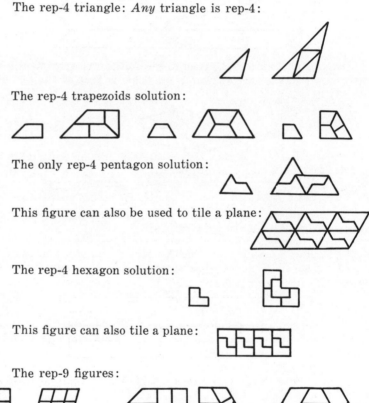

The rep-4 hexagon solution:

This figure can also tile a plane:

The rep-9 figures:

SQUARE   RHOMBUS   THREE REP-4 TRAPEZOIDS

The rep-4 pentagon is *not* rep-9. The rep-4 hexagon is rep-9:

6. THE SURPRISING MOEBIUS BAND

A Moebius band cut down the middle: It is the same as a regular band with two twists. It has two edges and two sides and is orientable.

A Moebius band cut one third of the way from the edge: Surprisingly, you will finish with *two* bands. One, with only one side, is a Moebius band that is the same length as the original band and the other, with two sides, is a regular band that is twice as long as the original. The second surprise is that the two bands are looped, like this:

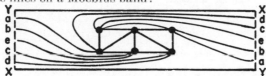

A Moebius band cut one quarter of the way from the edge: Again you get two linked bands, one of which is a Moebius band the same length as the original. The other band is regular, but twice as long.

Solution to the houses and utilities problem connected with telephone lines on a Moebius band:

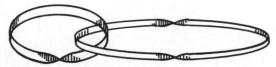

Coloring a map on the Moebius band: You will find that the least number of colors you can use is six (each number represents a color):

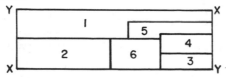

Solution to the second Moebius band map: Again at least six colors are needed:

Band with many twists: You will find that any band with an *odd* number of twists is a Moebius band with just one side and one edge. Any band with an *even* number of twists will be a regular band with two edges and two sides.

7. RUBBER SHEET FIGURES AND GENUS

Genus classes for capital letters:

GENUS 0 : CLMNSUVWZIJEFGHTHIKX
GENUS 1 : ARRDOPQ
GENUS 2 : BQ

Genus classes for small letters:

GENUS 0 : clsuvwzijftxkhnrym
GENUS 1 : aebdgpqo

Genus classes for numerals:

GENUS 0 : 123574
GENUS 1 : 4690
GENUS 2 : 8

Genus classes for capital Greek letters:

GENUS 0 : ΓΕΖΗΙΚΛΜΝΞΠΣΤΥΧΨΩ
GENUS 1 : ΑΔΟΡ
GENUS 2 : ΒΘΦ

Genus classes for small Greek letters:

GENUS 0 : εηικλμνπτυχψω
GENUS 1 : αγδςορσ
GENUS 2 : βθφξ

Genus classes for capital Russian letters:

GENUS 0 : ЖЗИЛЦЧШЭ
GENUS 1 : БДЪЮЯ

Genus classes for small Russian letters (same letters as for capitals in each) :

GENUS 0 : жзилцчшэ
GENUS 1 : бдъюя

Betti numbers for the four networks:

Betti number for the Moebius band: Only one cut is needed to make the band of genus zero, so the Betti number is one.

Turning an unbuttoned vest inside out with hands clasped in front of you: Lift the vest over your head so that it will hang on your arms, then turn it inside out through the armholes and return it over your head so that you have it on again. It takes some practice!

122

8. DOTS AND LINES IN THE AIR

Loop with a buttoned vest: Take the loop through the left armhole of the vest, get it over your head, then out through the other armhole and over the other arm and back through the right armhole. The loop will then circle your chest beneath the vest. Just slip it down to your waist and down your legs and step out of the loop.

9. POLYHEDRON PROBLEMS

Tracing the edges of polyhedrons with Hamiltonian or Eulerian paths: *All* the polyhedrons can be traced with a Hamiltonian path, but *none* with an Eulerian path.

Euler's formula for concave polyhedrons: The following is a list of the vertices, faces, and edges of the four figures:

	V	F	E
first	10	9	17
second	12	10	20
third	10	12	20
fourth	13	13	24

You can see that the value for the formula is still 2 for all four polyhedrons.

Euler's formula for polyhedrons with holes in them: The following is a list of the V, F, and E for the two figures:

	V	F	E
first	10	7	15
second	14	9	21

Again, Euler's formula still has the value of 2 for each figure.

Coloring the octahedron with the least number of colors:

You see that only two colors are needed.

Coloring the flattened dodecahedron and icosahedron with the least number of colors (each number represents a color):

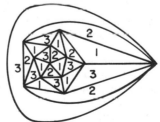

123

Solution to connecting the rest of the six points on a torus (A to C, and B to D):

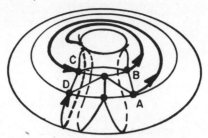

Solution to the network problem on a torus:

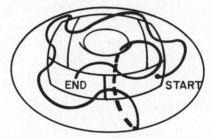

There is no solution to the network with the hole of the torus in any other region except the one above.

Solution to the complicated map on the torus:

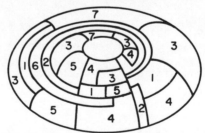

You see that only seven colors still are needed.

Euler's formula for the three toruses with maps:

	R	V	E
first	4	4	8
second	8	8	16
third	9	9	18

Euler's formula for these toruses is still zero in each case.

Betti number for the triple torus: Since only six cuts are required, the Betti number is six.

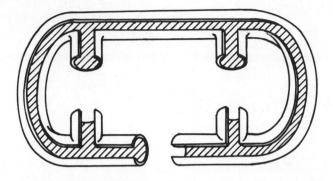

Bibliography

The following books provided background information for various chapters.

Barr, Stephen, *Experiments in Topology*. Thomas Y. Crowell Company, 1964.
Hilbert, David, and Cohn-Vossen, Stephan, *Geometry and the Imagination*, translated by P. Nemenyi. Chelsea Publishing Company, Inc., 1952.
Lietzmann, Walther, *Visual Topology*, translated by M. Brockheimer. American Elsevier Publishing Company, Inc., 1965.

In addition to books, the following articles supplied information.

Scientific American, "Mathematical Games," Martin Gardner, November, 1957 (p. 140); October, 1958 (p. 124); September, 1960 (p. 218); October, 1960 (p. 172); September, 1961 (p. 242); July, 1963 (p. 134); April, 1964 (p. 126); May, 1964 (p. 118); March, 1965 (p. 112); April, 1965 (p. 128); November, 1965 (p. 116); December, 1965 (p. 100); December, 1968 (p. 112).
Scientific American, "Topology," N. W. Tucker and H. S. Bailer, January, 1950 (p. 18).
Scripta Mathematica, Vol. 17, "Topology and Magic," Martin Gardner, 1951 (p. 75).

Index